Metamorphosis

Freedom and Transformation
through the Cross

EMMA LYNN GLICK

with foreword by Jennifer Weber

CROSSBOOKS
PUBLISHING

CrossBooks™
A Division of LifeWay
1663 Liberty Drive
Bloomington, IN 47403
www.crossbooks.com
Phone: 1-866-879-0502

First published by CrossBooks 11/12/2013

ISBN: 978-1-4627-2772-8 (sc)
ISBN: 978-1-4627-2773-5 (e)

Printed in the United States of America.

This book is printed on acid-free paper.

Any people depicted in stock imagery provided by Thinkstock are models,
and such images are being used for illustrative purposes only.

Certain stock imagery © Thinkstock.

Scripture taken from the King James Version of the Bible.

Contents

Foreword

There seem to be many various theories out there which attempt to explain the formation of a diamond. In all these theories there are these common strands that are agreed upon: carbon, heat, and pressure. Carbon, an element found on the periodic table, is an atom that forms many things on our earth including diamonds. There are so many minerals, organic compounds, and even gases that contain carbon. Because coal is primarily a form of carbon it is often believed that diamonds have been formed in the earth when coal, or another carbonic rock is subjected to extreme temperatures and pressure over time. Then heat and pressure are the factors determining whether carbon will appear as a rock barely worth anything, or a diamond, worth a considerable monetary sum.

Let's now consider the amazing diamond. Diamonds thought of for the rare beauty or the stone. With the right cuts made to be clear stone, it is capable of reflecting a rainbow of brilliant colors while being clear. This makes it a very nice decoration for a woman's finger. However this is not the primary reason that a diamond is worn in an engagement ring. As the hardest mineral on earth we can say it is the toughest and most durable. Nothing can scratch or cut a diamond except another diamond. When a man wants to win over a woman to be his mate and the love of his life, he chooses a symbol of lasting endurance, which cannot be changed, to represent the kind of love he will show throughout the marriage if she will have him as her husband. And of course he makes a small sacrifice of hard earned money to buy the expensive ring. The diamond's monetary value comes from its rarity and qualities. These qualities that distinguish it among other forms of carbon are achieved through heat and pressure.

So heat and pressure turn an ordinary carbonic rock into a precious gem. Essentially the same materials, it is the process and the change that makes all of the difference. This idea of transformation seen in nature is not limited to only non-living things. There is another example from nature that I think of. We often teach it to children and overlook the awe and life applications that can be drawn from the transformation a caterpillar endures in the process of becoming a butterfly.

Let's for a moment contrast the features of the creature at each stage of life. While a caterpillar, flight is impossible. After transformation, a butterfly has wings enabling it to fly. Even the legs, eyes and antennae undergo changes in the metamorphosis. A caterpillar is not known for any kind of beauty, but once a butterfly its beauty is admired by many. It is suddenly characterized by a delicate gracefulness since emerging from the chrysalis as a new creature.

So there are just two instances in nature where we can see that a process of change produces the most wonderful results. This can be us too if we are willing to be transformed. This book which you are about to read is all about transformation. We are promised that we can be a new creature. (**2 Corinthians 5:17** therefore, if anyone is in Christ, the **new** creation has come: the old has gone, the **new** is here!) Once we are born again we have become justified through the blood of Christ and we are a new creature.

I mentioned earlier that a butterfly can fly after its wings are developed but that is only partially true. It takes about an hour from the time the insect emerges from the hard shell of the chrysalis stage until it can fly. It must wait for its wings to be pumped full of hemolymph, the blood-like substance of an insect. In this hour it is very vulnerable to predators until it can finally fly. We are like that butterfly. We are a new creature and yet there is still work to be done in us for growth. We are to be transformed daily through the renewing of our minds. (**Romans 12:2**) I know I desperately need to be refined and made new daily through the process of sanctification.

I pray that the book you are about to read will inspire you toward greater transformation in your life and may you experience the greatest transformation possible if you haven't already. Jesus wants to give you His Holy Spirit which will work in you with Divine power. How would that look on a "Life is Good" T-shirt I wonder?

Jennifer Weber

Preface

The beauty of transformation. It is captivating, inspiring and it happens everywhere. Transformation requires a process. A process that takes time. The thing that amazes me the most about transformation is the way messes become miracles or things unattractive become extremely fascinating.

My favorite part of being an interior painter is the transformation that takes place. It can be the worst place, with me wanting to walk away and refer to them another painter, but with the right tools in the right place, with lots of work and a process, I end up wanting to live there. The cold and bare becomes warm and homelike. The end result is worth every piece of effort and work put into it. And I was also always intrigued at "metamorphosis." The process of a caterpillar changing into a butterfly.

Most of all, more than a room or a worm being changed, I love seeing lives changed by the blood of Jesus. It amazes me what happens to a heart that is given to the Lord. The hand of God on a heart of stone is powerful. When one of us is willing to take on Christ and lay before God our very own heart, He takes that which is laid before Him and does miracles.

I was inspired by my God to write "Metamorphosis." He laid it on my heart when I was in the mountains, surrounded by all He created. It was one of those what I call "forever moments." It was a perfectly gorgeous day and I was alone in His presence. I felt in a quiet yet very profound way, "write." I was stunned and like, "what?!

What shall I write? Everything is already written in Your Word. "What can I do?" "Metamorphosis" I instantly heard in my heart.

I argued, I battled and I questioned. But it just didn't go away. So I decided, "ok, I'll give it a try." Now, almost 3 years later, by the grace of the Most High, it is in completion. It has been an exciting, scary, and an overwhelming journey.

I am praying and hoping that as you read, you are encouraged in your walk with God, you will desire more of Him and His transformation in your life, and that your bondages become breakthroughs.

Or if you do not know Him, I pray you will get to know Him. What He has to offer is more exciting than anything that exists. No matter how messed up your life is, because of the cross, He can turn that mess into a miracle. He will take your chains and give you complete freedom. All glory and honour to Him Who reigns on high, Who is in heaven yet abiding here with us. Who is alive and preparing a place for His people to dwell with Him, free forever.

Yes, He is good. Yes, He is real. He loves you and has a purpose for you. MAY HIS GRACE GIVE YOU COURAGE TO BELIEVE IN THAT EVERY SINGLE DAY . . .

Emma Lynn Glick

Acknowledgements

Thank you to my Father, my King, my Redeemer, for reaching down into my sin and shame and setting me free by Your blood. Thank you for making this book possible. Thank you for walking with me and allowing me to experience You and wrap myself in Your love.

Thank you Dad and Mom. For loving me and giving me a beautiful life at home. And for giving me the best gift of all, guidance to our Lord and King.

Wayne, always my big brother, always my hero. You have set an example of strength and truth in Him, and I am forever grateful for having you to look up to.

Malena, Anna Mae, Rosa, Bethany. My beautiful sisters, my best friends, my soulmates. You have loved me and accepted me. Through the good and the rough, you have been there. Thank you. I love you's so much.

Carolyn, you believed in me. You listened and understood. You have encouraged me and given me new perspective so many times. Thank you.

Kay, you have brought hope into my darkest places. Thank you for counseling me, for praying for me and for speaking truth into my life.

Ruth Marie, thank you for being my motivator and encouraging me to "keep writing." Thank you for sharing your beautiful testimony. Most of all, thank you for being the friend you are. From the crazy times to deep heart to heart times, thank you for being that person in my life.

And to all my friends. My incredible gifts from God. My sisters in Him. Thank you for praying for me, encouraging me and for loving me. I love you all so much and cannot imagine life without you all.

Jen, thank you for writing the foreword. I am so excited to have it as part of the book.

Daniel Luke. Thank you so much for who you are. For encouraging me and pouring life into my heart. Thank you for showing me what love from God really is. I appreciate you, I love you and I am so grateful for the gift you are.

Thank you to everyone at Crossbooks. Thank you for being faithful, trustworthy and dependable.

And to YOU reader, may you be blessed, encouraged and find hope in the pages ahead.

1

From Darkness To Light

Waters flowed over my head, then I said, "I am cut off." I called upon Thy name, oh Lord. Out of the low dungeon, Thou hast heard my voice. "Hide not thine ear at my breathing, at my cry." Thou drewest near in the day that I called upon Thee. You said, "fear not." Oh Lord, You have pleaded the causes of my soul. YOU HAVE REDEEMED MY LIFE . . . Lamentations 3:54-58

I am in a room. A room so thick with darkness, I don't see a thing. I can feel the darkness, as if I could cut it with a knife. It is saturating me and suffocating me. It has been so long that I've seen light, I can hardly remember what light even is. I just know that I want it. Desperately.

So I search. Frantically looking for a way of escape from this cold, empty dungeon. Running my hands on the floor, along the walls, and as high as I can reach. I discover many doors and windows. Relief washes over me. Surely, there is light behind them.

I also discover one large door bolted shut. I give it a push, then a shove, trying with everything I have to get it open. It doesn't budge.

The other doors and windows don't seem quite as complicated and hard. None of them seem latched and some are even swinging wide open.

Hoping to find light I begin to search, feeling my way around. All I can see is pitch black darkness. Groping my way through the inky dark, I think I find a door of escape. I go through and stumble into more darkness. I come to another and the same thing happens. Over and over, it happens. Another, what I thought was an escape, brings me to more darkness.

I'm pushing and shoving through an endless maze of halls, chambers, tunnels, doors, and windows. The dark leading to darker, I am getting nowhere.

I motivate myself, "one more door. One more try. Surely I will find freedom." I hear noise. Sounds I try to follow, but everything blends together making it impossible to focus or make any sense of it.

On and on I stumble, desperately trying to find my own way out. Disappointed with every attempt, I'm getting extremely frustrated. I am exhausted and hungry. My throat is parched and I need rest and peace.

As I find myself in a pit of despair, hitting rock bottom, I have an idea. "I can go back to the beginning and start over on a different route."

So with the little strength I have left, I make an effort to backtrack to the beginning. Angry at all the wrong turns and deceiving doorways of escape that got me here, I weakly turn the opposite way. It is then I realize I have no idea where I am. Not even the slightest clue. I don't even know how on earth I got here.

Determined to find my own way back, I keep trying. I stumble and fall continuously, failing miserably every time.

I fall into a slimy mud hole and I can't get up. I'm done. I give up. My life is over. All hope is gone and every ounce of motivation has left my being. I am one big mistake. I am helpless and broken. As I lie there in anguish and disappointment, I'm listening to the sounds. Desperately straining my ears to maybe make sense of something.

Then I hear something. A sound blended in with all the other noise, yet very distinct and different. It sounds like knocking or some sort of faint tapping. A very appealing sound to me in that moment.

I try to get up but can't, so I crawl. Dragging my body through the dirt and mud, I search for the sound. For a long time I continue groping around in the darkness, following the sound. It continues, becoming more distinct and louder. I am getting closer and closer.

Suddenly I find myself lying in front of the big door. Remembering this door with its bolts and locks, I groan in disappointment. "I am too weak to open it. It's chained, it's bolted and the lock is sealed. It is impossible. I have tried." So I sit, helplessly facing this gigantic door. The knocking is becoming more rapid and intense, echoing through the entire place. It is now the only sound I hear.

My heart is pumping, all else is fading away and my only focus is on the door in front of me. "Surely he has keys! Surely he can get me out of here!" Anxiously I wait, but nothing happens. I muster up a little strength and drag myself to the door. I push myself against it in vain.

In pain and agony I cry out, hoping to be heard and somehow helped.

In one miraculous moment, I hear the jangle of keys. The latch turns and the door cracks open. A streak of light enters the room becoming brighter by the second.

I wait in anticipation and excitement as the door opens completely. I now feel uncomfortable and somewhat afraid. It is so bright, yet feels so good.

There, in the wide open doorway, I see Him. He is standing with His arms wide open. In a pile beside Him are the bolts, chains, and locks that kept the door closed.

Lying in the dirt I weakly attempt to get up. Finding it impossible I fall back, sinking into the mud.

He steps forward, closer to me, and stretches forth His hands, waiting for me to take them.

As I reach up to receive His embrace, I am suddenly very aware of something. Terrified and ashamed, I jerk my hands back. I just saw how very filthy and grimy they are. The light coming off of Him is making everything visible. I then dare to look at my feet. They are blistered, calloused and also filthy. My clothes are in shreds and I am covered in a reeking muck from head to toe. It is dripping off of me, creating the pool I'm lying in. The stench is repulsive and unbearable.

I know I am now completely revealed to Him. He sees it all, nothing hidden. Everything I am and the disgusting place I've been dwelling in. He sees all the darkness. Every wrong turn I've made. Every stupid mistake. He sees the dirt, muck and slime. He sees all the hidden chambers covered in dust and cobwebs. He sees all the doors I have tried for freedom. He sees how weak and pathetic I have become. I am completely contaminated, infected, unclean, and a disgrace to behold. I reek and am tainted, bruised and scarred. There is not an ounce of anything beautiful about me.

Disgusted and disappointed, I force my body to turn away. I am sure He will never accept me like this. He could never want me or help me. I can't even stand myself, how could anyone else? I don't deserve to be free. I'm way too covered in my own filth. As I crawl away defeated, I head back toward the slime. I glance longingly over my shoulder one last time, expecting Him to be gone.

But He is still standing there. His piercing eyes of pure love are gazing upon me. His arms are still wide open and He is now inside the door. Tears are streaming down His cheeks and making impact in the pool of muck.

He is reaching out, waiting for me to return. Pleading with me He says, "my child, come. Come to me. I love you because I know you. You are mine. You belong to me."

I cry out, "but You are perfect. You are beautiful and pure. I am filthy, pathetic and unworthy. I am nothing."

He replies with a voice of tender mercy and strength, "without me you are. But that is the reason I have come. I have not come to condemn you or reject you, but to set you free and claim you for my Kingdom. I will cleanse you. I will give you new clothes and a new home. I will satisfy your hunger and quench your thirst. I will make you new and walk with you forever."

Weeping, I surrender and receive His embrace. He picks me up, wraps His arms of love around me and carries me. He does exactly as He has promised and teaches me to walk in His light and love, free forever.

"Come now, let us reason together," saith the Lord. Though your sins be as scarlet, they shall be white as snow. Though they be red like crimson, they shall be as wool. Isaiah 1:18

2

Freedom

I waited patiently for the Lord, and He inclined unto me and heard my cry. He brought me up also out of a horrible pit, out of the miry clay, (swampy earth) and set my feet upon a rock, and established my goings. He hath put a new song in my mouth, even praise unto our God. Psalm 40.

Freedom. The state of being free. At liberty rather than in confinement or under restraint. The absence of or release from ties, obligations, bondage or slavery. Ease of movement or action. The right to enjoy all the privileges or special rights of citizenship or membership.

Just the sound of the word "freedom" sends some kind of tingling or adrenaline through my being. Anything to feel free or to be free motivates me.

We thrive on freedom. America cries, "let freedom ring." This doesn't mean let it ring with a quiet whisper or a soft tone. It means, "let it echo across the land, to the end of the earth." A ring is a continuous sound. Ongoing and powerful. The phone rings. The doorbell rings. It's a sound that makes impact, grabbing your attention.

That's exactly what the ringing of freedom does to the soul. It's captivating and snatches all attention. We were created to live in freedom. Freedom in Christ. God put an intense desire for freedom deep within our souls. This is why we search diligently for anything to find freedom. Anything that makes us feel free and powerful.

We have the mentality that freedom is an all-powerful, invincible, "I can do anything I want, how I want, where I want, when I want," state of being. When we feel in control we think we are living in freedom. When we walk in our own way, making our own choices, living life with tunnel vision, focused on me and what I want, we feel free.

"I have needs, I have rights and I deserve it," is what we think freedom is. The freedom of choice and the freedom of speech dominate our minds. Rights. The right to say what he needs to hear because "he needs to be put in place." The right to give up on the marriage because it's "just too hard." The right to refuse to forgive because "they don't deserve my forgiveness."

We grope around in darkness seeking out freedom, falling into more darkness.

"It's my body, I can use it how I want." So we have one night stands because it gives a sense of freedom and fulfillment. Then comes the pregnancy. Again, "it's my body and I don't want a baby." We reject a soul that's been created by God. We get the abortion and try to forget about it. We were not created to forget about it. Anything tied that deep emotionally will never go away. We feel bound to the pain, so we search harder to make it go away. More darkness.

We think the opposite sex will never understand and we only feel connected to the same gender. We think it's ok because "it's my body, my life, and I can't help it."

No, we can't help it. But there is One who can. He can do a whole lot more than help. He heals and He transforms. He brings victory and restoration into any area of defeat and devastation.

We think we have the freedom of speech so we verbally express everything we feel. We hate, we cut and we destroy with our tongues. The power of "life and death" lie in our tongues. We can kill someone's spirit or bring them to life. Sadly, many times, because of what we think is a "right," we kill. We gossip, we lie, we tear people down to lift ourselves up. We flatter with lying lips to bring ourselves to being liked. Honesty is way too risky.

We keep searching for life and freedom. Something to numb the pain. Just one more time we go to that bar. We need that drink. We need that high. "It's the last time," we promise ourselves. But it happens again and again.

All money is spent on our addictions. "It's my money. I can spend it how I want." We hoard it. Needing it all for ourselves, forgetting about the neighbor who has a hospital bill and has just lost his job.

We use our own sick lusts on innocent people and destroy their lives. But we don't care. It felt good.

We refuse to forgive for if we do, we would lose the upper hand and be giving in to them. "My emotions are mine. I can stay mad if I want to." Emotional stress and anxiety grip our souls, causing nerves to go weird and blood pressure to rise. Emotional sickness causes physical sickness. They are tied together. Depression brings us to a place so low it's almost impossible to find a way out.

All this because "we are on our own and we are free." We don't need help or advice. We don't want to surrender our EVERYTHING. It's too risky and way too uncomfortable. Releasing control feels too much like a weakling. Letting go of our own self will seems too wimpy and soft. We need to hang on to what feels strong, powerful and free.

So we stumble around in the dark, empty and lost. Hungry, with parched throats. Miserable, covered in our own muck and sin that controls our life.

What feels like freedom to the flesh, is spiritual bondage. It is being so bound and controlled by all these strongholds, we are too blind to see our own chains. We search for what we think is the easy way, but in spiritual reality it's the hardest way.

This, what we call freedom and rights in ourselves, will not last forever. It will pass away. There is only One Way to eternal freedom. There is only One who can bring all things to light and transform you and set you free. His name is Jesus. He offers freedom that can start right now and never end. He offers the best way, the real authentic way to life. The way that will bring you rest, peace and healing.

Once you experience just a taste of His Glory, it will have you amazed, intrigued and hungry for more. If you continue to drink from His fountains of living waters and receive what He has to offer, it will satisfy you and deeply fulfill you. It will shed light into your dark world and pull you out of the swamp.

The first step to freedom has already been taken. The map has been drawn, the path trod. The sacrifice has been made, the blood shed. The punishment for your sin has already been taken place. The debt is paid.

You cannot do it yourself. You cannot set yourself free. Try and you will fail.

Jesus death and resurrection is an invitation that has already been proclaimed. He did it for you, He did it for me. Everything that needed to take place to make freedom possible, was done by Jesus. So as you grope around in darkness, searching for love and security, desperately looking for a way out or pain relief, He is standing at the door of your prison with His arms wide open. He is calling your name. His tears are dripping into the pool of your pain, for His heart is breaking at what is happening to His precious child. He already knows you and loves you and is waiting for you to return to Him. He formed you and calls you His own, therefore He wants you with Him. He made a way out because He knows you need Him, desperately.

Until you also realize your desperate need for Him, you will never experience true freedom. He will not force His way into your life. The next step to freedom is yours to take. It is your choice to make, your shot to call. He holds the key to your heart. The heart He created. He is pursuing you, trying to get your attention. Are you listening? Or are you distracted by everything around you, not hearing His call or feeling His nudge? He will allow things into your life to bring to your attention the fact that you need a stronger arm around you. Holding you, protecting you and giving you life.

Yes, He holds the keys. The only keys that fit into the lock of your heart. But He will not come in without an invitation or permission. You have already been chosen by Him. He is already crazy in love with you. He is waiting for you to take that step towards His freedom and love. No one can do it for you. Don't wait on your friends or your family. It may look hard and complicated, maybe even impossible, leaving all else behind to come and follow Him. If you wait till it looks easy, you will miss it. That time of taking the luxurious road to freedom will never come. Jesus did not wait till it was easy to die for you. He did not die a soft, luxurious death. It was hardcore. The only way for Him to do the impossible was by surrendering to the will of His Father and allowing God to work in Him. And so goes for you. This step that needs to be taken cannot be done by you alone. Yes, you need to choose it, but only Christ in you can make it possible. What looks hard, complicated, and impossible right now can very easily and perfectly be done by Him who loves you and died for you.

He sees where you have been, what you have done, and who you have become. Again I say, He is waiting, seeing it all. Respond to His Presence and He will open that gigantic, chained and bolted door of your prison that always looked so hard. Surrender to Him and He will shatter all you've become. He will shed marvelous light onto your place of shame and pick you up out of the slime. He will carry you away from the filth. He will cleanse you, clothe you, transform you and teach you to walk, free forever.

3

Infinite Grace

I've heard that one of the best things you can share with someone is your testimony of what God has done in your life. A testimony is used, not to magnify what I have done, but to bring to light and magnify what "God has done."

I titled this "infinite grace" because really, that's what He poured into my life of sin. Infinite, boundless, unlimited grace. Without it, I would be doomed. It was His grace that brought me salvation and freedom in Him.

Psalm 73:22-26 says "so foolish was I and ignorant, I was as a beast before Thee. Nevertheless, I am continually with Thee. Thou hast held me by my right hand, Thou shalt guide me with Thy counsel, and afterward receive me to glory. Whom have I in heaven but Thee? And there is none upon earth that I desire beside Thee. My flesh and my heart faileth, but God is the strength of my heart and my portion forever" . . .

Beautiful words of promise. We need a Saviour to love on us and to save us from the evil one. Without Him, we are lost and pathetic. With Him, we have a strength to live off of forever.

For a long time I didn't understand this. I always knew I needed Him, but not to the full extent of how much I actually do.

11

I thought I need to somehow "do good enough or do some kind of good work" to attain freedom. I tried to find my own way out of sin, searching for freedom and failing miserably. I did not understand or realize the fullness and depth of God's infinite grace. I didn't know "why" I do the things I do. My works were used to try to gain favor of God. I thought I need to be good, go to church and do what's right because I am a Christian. What I didn't understand is that works are a "result" of a relationship with Him. A relationship is not formed by trying to be "good" all the time. The relationship and an understanding of grace needs to be formed before trying anything else.

I didn't know how much God really loves me and how He wanted me to understand He is the ONLY way to salvation. I couldn't find my own way there. He wanted me to need Him so desperately I would stop trying to do it on my own and surrender it ALL to Him. What God wanted from me, because he knew that's what is best for His children, was complete dependence on Him. I needed to come to Him with ALL MY HEART. He wanted me, and all of me to Himself. Not just a part of me on Sunday morning or daily devotions, but every ounce of me laid down at the foot of the cross. But I didn't "get" that for quite a while.

I was living for Jesus one minute and myself the next. I would confess and try to receive His love, but I kept doing exactly how I wanted. Surrendering my entire everything was just too hard.

There were things I didn't pray about because I was scared to bring them into the light or I enjoyed them too much to give them up. I tried to live out in faith, but basically lived a life of chaotic up and down, feeling empty and insecure most of the time. I would be on top of, or think I am on top of things for a while and the next thing I knew I was back in a rut, just living my selfish, mediocre life. It's all about me and what I wanna do.

I was extremely dependant on other people to give me a sense of security. I did things for people to gain approval and looked to them for fulfillment.

I often felt like a failure because I was disappointed with myself for messing up all the time. I blamed the people around me for everything to ease me of the guilt that I carried from messing up all the time. I was very defensive, building walls around my heart to keep it protected from any kind of accusation or correction from others. I hated feeling condemned and did whatever it took to prevent feeling it. But it was done in a very unhealthy way.

I searched for love and security in all the wrong places, coming up empty every time. I fell continuously, learning lesson after lesson. Making confession after confession.

I kept God at arm's length. Yes I desired Him and spent time with Him. But it never lasted long enough or went deep enough to really change my life. I would go right back to God "there" and me "here." A wall between us. Distance.

My parents taught me about Jesus and I accepted Him when I was a little girl. I had a wonderful family and super friends. I was blessed but as I grew older and got into my teenage years, there was something huge missing. That something was, "peace that surpasses all understanding." A peace straight from the floodgates of mercy. The peace that floods the soul and gives complete knowing of God's presence in the heart. It was not to be found. I was discontent, restless and very impatient. I didn't know why my joy never lasted. It felt like I was chasing after a butterfly that kept getting away.

The things I went to for security and fulfillment felt so good. They controlled my life and I couldn't let go. There were things I needed to stop trying to control but didn't want to. I didn't want to be vulnerable. Being vulnerable felt weak, and feeling weak was too risky and dangerous.

I was living a very mediocre life. A life with two roads. I was trying to serve God and at the same time I kept crawling in filth that bogged me down and hindered me from God's fullness. That was messed up, chaotic, and it was sin.

There were many times I did things impulsively because I wanted to fit in or I was too weak to say no. Most times though, it felt good and gave me a sense of freedom or power. I would plan to do things I knew were wrong. I didn't have the courage to turn around and walk away. Weekends I stayed up all night, getting into junk. Arriving home just in time to sleep a little before going to church. I barely stayed awake enough to receive the message.

I was miserable and too blind to even know I was. Sunday nights after the weekend, I came home and confessed, regretting everything I did. I would try to make up for it by reading my Bible and trying to pray.

The next weekend would be a repeat of the weekend before.

I finally came to a point where I knew I needed something different and wanted more. So I committed my life to Christ and got baptized. That was a big turning point in my life. God became very real to me and His grace was sufficient.

But I withheld so much. I just couldn't lay it all down. It was too much to give every single piece of myself to Him. I still wanted to make my own decisions and do things my own way. I wanted to keep hanging on to all the unhealthy things that felt good and gave me security.

Then God brought me to a year of hard time. Like really hard stuff unlike anything I had ever experienced before. I stood by as people I loved passed into eternity, and then looked upon their precious faces in caskets.

A relationship that my heart was depending on, failed.

These were people and relationships that I was attached to and couldn't imagine life without. I was stripped of things I built my life around and stored hope upon. My heart was broken like never before and shattered into pieces. I wondered when I would feel happiness again, or if there even was anything like happiness.

After walking through a lot of pain, anger, frustration and trying to find joy, I came to a place of being spent. My emotions were exhausting. I had hurts I could never heal on my own. I desperately wanted joy and peace I knew I could never find alone.

I then knew I needed to surrender. I couldn't do it anymore. I was tired of trying to work everything out "my way." I needed to allow God to saturate my soul and take over every piece of my entire life. It was time for me to stop telling God what I want and start asking Him what it is He wants. Stop with all my own good ideas and start listening to His. Stop hanging on to these shreds that I called valuable and receive what only He has to offer.

It was time for me to come to Him with nothing hidden, holding nothing back. I needed to give Him not only me, but also everything about me. Every breath I breathe. Every step I take. Every choice I make. Every thought I think. From the deepest, darkest parts of the hidden places in my soul to the most visible areas in my heart. It was time for me to hand it over to my Creator. It was time to give to Him all that I called mine and allow Him to transform it and make it His. I finally realized trying to find my own way into His arms will never work. I finally understood the only way into His arms was, "Him picking me up and carrying me." All I needed to do was surrender and allow Him to pour His infinite grace upon my wounded soul.

God revealed to me how desperately I needed Him and how pathetic I am on my own. He offered me His arms, His waiting outstretched arms. He gave me a second chance. A chance to allow Him to make it all new.

I accepted His offer and allowed Him to pick me up and carry me away from a life controlled by sin. He carried me onto the path of freedom in Him and Him alone. When He did this, my world shattered in the most awesome way. Things happened. He gave me new life, new motivations, and new desires. I felt like a brand new person. He revealed Himself to me in a way like never before and taught me new things of Himself. Things that had been valuable to me faded out. Things that I had been shrugging off became important.

He showed me that His will for my life is for me to abide in Him and He in me with nothing in between. All power, glory, majesty, praise and honor belong to the King on High. For He is good and His infinite grace never runs dry.

Because of that grace and because of the cross, He went from being at arm's length to sweeping me off my feet in His embrace.

He does this to those who come to Him. He did it for me, He will do it for you.

Infinite grace. Let it sink in. Embrace the newness and the purity of it. Let it wash over you every time you come to the foot of the cross with your heart wide open. Drink of it for it never runs out. Wash yourself in it and it will cleanse you like none other. Make it your lifeline and all you depend on. His infinite grace and His alone.

4

Metamorphosis

What fellowship hath righteousness with unrighteousness? What communion hath light with darkness? What harmony hath Christ with Satan? What part hath he that believes with an infidel (unbeliever)? What agreement hath the temple of God with idols? For ye are the temple of the living God. As God has said, "I will dwell in them, and walk in them. And I will be their God and they shall be my people. Wherefore, come out from among them and be separate," saith the Lord, "and touch not the unclean thing. And I will receive you. And will be a Father unto you, and you shall be my sons and daughters," saith the Lord Almighty. Having therefore these promises, dearly beloved, let us cleanse ourselves from all filthiness of the flesh and spirit, perfecting holiness in the fear (awe, reverence, deep regard, honour) of God. 2 Corinth. 6:14-18, 7:1

It is one or the other. Once you experience the grace of God and allow Him to pick you up, there will be transformation. That's how our God works. That's what He delights in. He changes dark to light. He transforms what Satan did in your life to what God is doing in your life. He turns doubts and unbelief into believing and knowing.

Worries and fears into security and peace. He takes away the idols in His temple (you) and fills it with His Spirit.

Only if you are willing to go with Him will He stay with you. You cannot go with Him with one foot in the muck. God does not and will not abide in dark places. He wants to get you as far away as possible of what holds you in bondage. He wants to pull you out and take you to His new, glorious place.

He specializes in metamorphosis. Metamorphosis means "complete transformation." It is a marked change in appearance, character, condition or the way something functions. God says in **Isaiah 42:16, "and I will bring the blind by a way that they knew not; I will lead them in paths that they have not known: I will make darkness light before them, and crooked things straight. These things will I do unto them and not forsake them."**

It's impossible to stay stuck in the mud and slime of life after receiving Christ and falling in love with Him. With surrendering and giving your life to Him, comes transformation.

There's a few things in nature that experience metamorphosis. A maggot changing into a fly. A tadpole into a frog. My favorite is a caterpillar changing into a butterfly. Metamorphosis of a butterfly involves a few stages. Egg, caterpillar, cocoon, adult. Metamorphosis is a radical change in an animal as it grows. It is the entire process of how an egg ends up as a butterfly.

Think about it. Impossible. An ugly worm chopping up everything he can get ahold of to survive, turning into a butterfly. Aflight, beautiful, spreading pollen to produce flowers.

The amazing thing is what happens between the two stages of egg and butterfly. It is a process and does not happen in a moment.

Witnessing metamorphosis is one of my favorite childhood memories.

I especially had a fascination for worms and toads. I would go to the pond and search for tadpoles and after catching some I would keep them somewhere until they became toads. It totally amazed me.

My mom, brother, sisters and I would go to the garden searching for caterpillars. We searched among the greens near the dirt, in pursuit of the squirmy, dirt-crawling creatures.

After finding one, we put it in a jar, punching holes in the lid and giving it greens to eat. The jar set on the counter for what seemed like many days. After a while we noticed a change in the caterpillar. It stopped moving as if it were dead. Every day it continued to change, becoming more drastic.

Suddenly it was simply a brown bag hanging from the stick we had put in the jar. A few days later another change occurred. We got excited and watched it intently. Something was happening bigtime!!! The cocoon was like wiggling and being weird.

Very slowly and with much effort, the butterfly started to push itself out of the cocoon. Eyes wide, in awe and amazement we watched as it struggled until it finally slipped out completely.

There it was. Very weak and shaky, flopping around. A brand new creature. Complete, perfect and gorgeous. We gave it some time to become stronger and more stable. Then mom carefully put it in the palm of her hand and we took it outside to its new home. The big open world. It fluttered its wings and took flight. Unsteady at first but soon gaining confidence and doing what it was created to do.

A perfect new being, leaving behind all he ever knew. Entering a new life, transformed and set free.

This transformation that takes place in animals or insects is exactly what takes place in our human spirit when walking with Christ. **And be ye not conformed to this world, but be ye transformed by the renewing of your mind, that you may prove what is the good, and acceptable, and perfect will of God. Romans 12:2**

The only One who will renew your mind is Christ. By the renewing of your mind comes transformation.

This is not a one-time thing that happens in an instant. It is a process. A process that takes time. Until the day we die, we need to renew our minds in Him daily, and His transformation in us will not be complete until we meet Him face to face.

The most unusual and complicated part of metamorphosis is the stage when the caterpillar forms a cocoon and goes through amazing changes and emerges a butterfly. The female butterfly lays an egg on the type of plant the young caterpillar will eat. The caterpillar hatches from the egg about 6 days after being laid. These tiny creatures are ravenous and quickly begin to eat away at every leaf in sight. During this time of tremendous growth, the caterpillar sheds its skin several times, becoming stronger and longer each turn. The caterpillar will end up being almost two inches long at the end of this cycle. The caterpillar knows when it is time to spin a cocoon because it secretes certain hormones.

We, being humans and heirs of Adam and Eve, are born into a world of sin. Being born into a world of sin, we are sinners serving our flesh. We reach for everything good in sight, feasting on all we can find. We become more wrapped up and the grip of it becomes stronger and more powerful in our life. We, being sinnners, need a Savior and until we realize that, nothing will ever make sense. We will stay like a caterpillar all our life. Once we do realize it, it is then we know it is time to do something about it. What will you do with that knowing? Where will you take that realization? Will you try to shut it out or will you pay close attention to the prompting of the Holy Spirit?

The caterpillar reacts to the knowing through instinct. By spinning silk and forming a cocoon, the caterpillar makes a little shell in which it can form the pupa. The caterpillar finds a leaf to hang on upside down from and begins to cover itself with either two leaves wrapped in silken threads or a cocoon made entirely of silk.

The caterpillar is oblivious to everything around him and does not get distracted from doing exactly as he has been created to do. The pupa is what the caterpillar is called while changing into a butterfly. Once inside the protected space, the pupa forms and amazing changes occur. During this time, the entire structure of the caterpillar reforms. Including the building of two wings, a long tongue in which to drink and suck nectar, two antenna, and the body of a butterfly.

After the pupa stage the butterfly emerges. In the beginning, the butterfly's body is soft and weak. New butterflies will spend time beating their wings, growing stronger and becoming adapted. As the wings beat, their circulatory systems fill.

During this time they are easy prey because they have no defenses and are unable to fly. It takes about an hour before the new butterfly is ready to leave the pupa and begin its new life. Once the butterfly leaves the pupa, the adult will live and reproduce.

Beautiful transformation. A caterpillar to a butterfly. Once a butterfly, it does not eat the same food as it did when it was a caterpillar. It does not live in the same place. It doesn't spend its time the same way or hang out in the same places. If it would, it would die. It finds its life and breath from a completely different source. It finds purpose in totally something new.

If you truly experience the power of the grace of God, you will be astounded and want nothing to do with your old life. Change and transformation take place when you experience being loved by God and when the impact of that love starts affecting the core of who you are.

To be fully connected to Christ and to walk in the safety of His presence, something must be done after surrendering to Him. You must put a source of protection around yourself as God works transformation in your life. Move away from the people and things that have caused downfall in your life and get yourself in a different atmosphere. Spend time with godly people, become active in a church, and put effort into your time spent with God. Ask Him to provide this hedge of protection for you. Above all, seek His heart diligently. Read His Word of life and love He wrote for you, spend time talking to Him and listening to Him. He is the ultimate protector and with His protection around your heart, He will transform you into what He created you to be.

With Him in your life, your motivation, energy, desire and reason to live will be coming from an entirely different source than it did in your life without Him. As His transformation takes place in your heart, you will become a new creature and a new home. Allow God in you and you in Him change your life. Worship Him. Honor Him. Need Him. Obey Him. Cry out to Him in all your hurts and praise Him in your joys.

Come to Him, willing to be made new in Him, and He will give you wings.

5

In The Fullness Of His Love

LOVE. We hear it, we speak it, it's everywhere. But is it sinking in? So far and deep that it shakes you to the core? Are you receiving love from Father God and letting it sweep you off your feet, giving you new life daily?

I was, and still am working through a lot of healing and restoration, or better said, "God is working." He has been restoring things I was stripped of, healing wounds from past relationships and bringing miracles of life into parts of me that died. It has been feeling like I'm being remodeled and it hasn't always been very comfortable.

So I'm trying to be ok with being very vulnerable and surrendering to His hand, but I was missing a beat. I thought a lot about how much I love Jesus, and yes, I am crazy in love with Him. But I forgot to focus on a fact and embrace the truth of that fact. The fact that "He loves me."

I was speaking it into other people's lives and even writing about it. I knew He loves me, but it's an important part I didn't emphasize enough or fully apply to my own heart.

When God revealed that to me, I was sitting on our back porch enjoying the quiet and soaking up nature. There was beauty all around me and so many times that's when He comes through. In the midst of all He has made.

I was searching for scripture to put into this chapter about a Father's love. As it turns out, the chapter has changed a lot because of what He revealed to me as I was searching.

While the apostle Paul was in prison he wrote beautiful life-changing scripture. **"For this cause I bow my knees unto the Father of our Lord Jesus Christ, of whom the whole family in heaven and earth is named, that He would grant you, according to the riches of His glory, to be strengthened with might by His Spirit in the inner man. That Christ may dwell in your hearts by faith, THAT YOU, BEING ROOTED AND GROUNDED IN LOVE, MAY BE ABLE TO COMPREHEND WITH ALL SAINTS WHAT IS THE BREADTH, AND LENGTH, AND DEPTH, AND HEIGHT; AND TO KNOW THE LOVE OF CHRIST, WHICH PASSETH KNOWLEDGE, THAT YE MIGHT BE FILLED WITH ALL THE FULLNESS OF GOD. Now unto Him that is able to do exceeding abundantly ABOVE ALL that we ask or think, according to the power that worketh in us, unto Him be glory in the church by Jesus Christ throughout all ages, world without end. Amen."
Ephesians 3:14-21.**

Wow and wow and wow. Read it again and again until you get it. It took me a while. Being "filled with the fullness of God" is what I was searching and longing for. I wanted to experience everything He has to offer. Every restoration, every healing, every joy, forgiveness, and peace. I wanted to experience it all. I especially wanted freedom from the haunting of my past sin and hurts in relationships.

When I read that scripture, I came to realize I will never be able to experience the complete fullness of God until I comprehend the breadth, length, depth, and height of His love for me. I must "know" that He loves me. And even when we comprehend it or know it, it's even more than that!!!

The scripture says it "passeth knowledge," meaning, our brain, no matter how wise, cannot fathom it. But in the mind of the Spirit, we can get a glimpse of it. If we direct our hearts to His heart of love and choose to have faith in His love, we get a taste of it. And even when we do catch on to it, understand it and live off of it, we will never completely grasp how much He actually does love us until we meet Him.

Can you fathom the richness, the fullness, the beauty and the perfection of the love of your heavenly Father? Ask Him to open your heart to it and show you and fill you with it. Speak it to yourself over and over.

I can hardly come to grips with it. I think it's a process. As time goes on, it will sink deeper and become more ingrained into the heart. What God has in His heart is something that blows our minds. A love that stuns us and brings us to a place of marveling. A love so great and so good, once tasted will have us hooked.

We cannot experience any kind of freedom, forgiveness, renewal, healing, restoration, joy, peace, freedom, or transformation until we know that we are loved and chosen by the King who made heaven and earth and all within. It's impossible to be drenched by or live in the fullness of God until you comprehend how much He loves you. Like really loves you. And He is also able to do exceeding abundantly all that we ask or even think. Think about all the wildest dreams you have. The miracles you would like to see happen or even just the bad habits you wanna break. No matter how radical, God has the power to do it. He truly is a mighty God and again I say, "He loves you."

Last spring when I was on a prison crusade, a friend and I stayed in a motel room together. I was battling with the freedom thing and I didn't feel worthy to be called to minister to these people with all the yuck in my own life. We were discussing it and she said, "live like you are loved."

Wait, "what?" So profound, yet so deep and full of power.

Can you confidently grab ahold of that and claim that promise? "I am loved." If you do apply that promise to your heart, there are

25

many things that will change in the way you think, act, and even live. It will impact your life in a mighty way.

One major, it's a slap in the enemy's face. He brings feelings of condemnation, unworthiness and guilt into our hearts and it is amazing the things we do as a result of all those unhealthy lies that are put there by him. He doesn't want you to believe that you are loved by God. He wants us to be afraid of God, not fall in love with Him. He hates a love that is self-sacrificial and unconditional. That is what God's love is. The enemy has the world brainwashed on what love is. He delights in selfish, obsessive love that brings bondage. When we discover the love that flows from the heart of the Father, it brings us life. Anything with death is from Satan. Anything with life is from God. Applying the truth that you are loved brings life and freedom. Staying in denial of that love will kill your inner spirit. Maybe not in a very obvious way, but there are parts of your soul that will shrivel away without you even knowing it.

I'm comparing a little bit, the love of God to the love of my daddy.

Now I know there are many people who do not know the love of an earthly Father, and if this is you, I am so sorry. Comparing the two would be an awful picture. There are many without a daddy or come from a broken home. Some have been abused, violently. Some have been hurt, mocked, criticized, belittled or never been told that he loves you. Our heavenly Father is nothing like that.

If you have had a tumultuous childhood with your dad, do not believe the lie that this is what God must be like. He is love. Pure, complete, unconditional, ever-lasting love. The deepest, most passionate emotion of love that exists, come from the heart of God. He has chosen you to be His child. He wants you to be covered in His love now and forever. He cares about you and loves you more than you could ever imagine or dream of. You are fearfully and wonderfully made by the work of His hands. He knows every thought, dream, emotion and affection that lies within your soul and He understands them when no one else does. And when you "just don't get it," He does. He knows what you are passionate about and what gets on your last nerve. The hair on your head is numbered by Him. He loves who you are, because who you are is who He created. And who He created when He made you, is exactly who He wants you to be. Your personality, your smile, the twinkle in your eyes, the color of your hair, eyes and skin. The sound of your voice, the way your tears streak up your face when you cry. From the shape of your eyebrows to the size of your toes, He specifically designed every detail. He's crazy in love with it all because it's you.

The Sovereign God, Almighty King wants to be connected to you. He wants your heart to be totally entwined with His. Wrapped up, involved and stedfast. He wants that kind of intimate relationship with you. He wants to give you way more than your daddy ever did. He is the ultimate Father. He wants to be a big deal to you. You are already a big deal to Him.

I am blessed with wonderful parents. My parent's love to me is a teeny tiny glimpse or idea of God's love to every soul on the planet.

A mother's love is a love unlike any other love. It's a love that lays aside things that once were important, to invest in her child's life. It's a love that cares more about her baby's comfort than her own. It's a love that takes the time to encourage her child to learn and grow. She teaches her things no one else can or would. It's a love that wants what is best for her child, and sometimes that means saying "no" and being a disappointment to her. It's a love that would die for her child's protection, safety or life. It's a love that carries her baby for 9 months, doing whatever necessary to keep the baby healthy and safe. It's a love that nurtures, feeds, protects, holds, cherishes, cuddles, spends time with, leads, guides, and teaches her baby. It's a love that holds her child when she is hurt or sick and joins in her child's delight in all the small things.

Her child, who is such a deep part of her, who she gave birth to, who is so deeply woven into the very depths of her own soul, the precious child is her own. Her child is her flesh and blood, a part of herself and very connected to her soul. As the child sleeps peacefully in the silent night, her precious face bathed in the warm moonlight, the Mother gazes upon her longingly and knows she will love her forever. No matter what decisions her baby will make, or how far she will roam, the Mother will always be waiting for her to return. The love flowing out of the Mother's heart and into her child's life, will never fade away. It will only grow. For she is the one she calls her own and their souls are destined to be connected forever.

My daddy always was and always will be my hero. As I was growing up, he really was my knight in shining armor. His strength in my life eased many burdens. From fixing my toys to wrapping his strong arms around me as I cried, he was there. I admired his strength. I loved it when he showed me his biceps. As he rolled up his sleeves and popped those muscles, my eyes grew wide, in total amazement. When he came home from work, I ran into his outstretched arms and he picked me up, threw me into the air and caught me again. He did it perfectly every time, never missing a beat. It was the most crazy thrilling experience and my favorite moment of the day. He gave the best bear hugs by wrapping his big, strong arms around my small body. He would squeeze the breath out of me. I in return, would try to do the same thing, but my tiny arms barely made a dent in his strong body. I thought he could do anything. I called him "my Mr. Fixerman." If I had a broken toy, I took it to him and he fixed it the best he could. To me it was perfection.

Summer evenings were spent in the backyard consisting of airplane rides, piggybacks, and daddy horseback rides. Again, it was his strength that captivated me. He was strong and powerful, but so gentle and kind. With my tiny hand in his, I felt safe and protected.

There are a couple different meanings of "fear." Fear: to regard with awe. To have reverential awe of God. This one is used many times in the Bible when talking about "fearing God." I feared my dad with this description of fear. His strength did not make me afraid, but gave me a sense of security and protection. Because he was much stronger than me I knew the power he had. That brought forth a fear, but a healthy fear.

When my parents punished me, I hated it. It hurt physically, but mostly broke my heart. They did it because they loved me and wanted me to learn that there are consequences when messing with doing what's wrong. That put a sense of respect in me. It formed a conscience and built conviction. It taught me to live in a sense of fear. Not the scared kind of fear, but a fear that gave me courage and motivated me to try and do the right thing.

When I accomplished something and showed mom or dad, or told them about it, the most important thing in that moment was their approval. Their praise. They were interested in what I did and helped me with projects, because they love me and cared about all the details in my life.

Recently I found a picture of my dad and me. We are sitting at the top of a slide, ready to go down. I was just a toddler, about one yr. old. Observing the picture, I imagined what went on in that moment. I probably wanted to go but felt afraid. Or maybe I would've even attempted to go alone, not seeing the danger, if dad wouldn't have been around to go with me. He could have told me how and given me direction, then stood back and waited for me at the bottom, coaching me the whole time. But no, he knew there was no way for me to go the trip alone. I was just a baby, his baby, and he didn't wanna see me get hurt. So he went with me. He held me, not just partially, but completely. His one arm is around me all the way, his other hand is gripping the side of the slide controlling the speed. He is in control and I am trusting him with no fear. (a distressing emotion aroused by impending danger, evil, pain, etc. dismay, dread, terror, fright, panic, horror.)

For I am in the arms of my daddy.

He never loses his hold on me and goes with me all the way.

My first trip to the beach consisted of my family going to Rehobeth beach, Deleware for the day. What a day. I was 6 and I'll never forget it. I loved the sand. Loved it so much I had too much on me and in me at the end of the day. The ride home was somewhat torturous. Anyway, I was scared of the waves, so I stayed at the water's edge. Somehow dad got me persuaded to go in with him. If I remember right, it took him awhile to get me convinced. I always had a hard time getting out of my comfort zone, and still do at times. He promised me we would be fine. "Don't worry, I got ya." So he picked me up and out we went into the vast unknown. Everything is going fine and I'm starting to actually kinda like it. Then suddenly, this enormous wave that took dad by complete surprise came up behind us, never giving us a chance to escape. He tried to jump it but it was too high. It crashed over us, immersing us completely. I was terrified and came up bawling and very upset. Dad felt terrible and he was so sorry. I didn't go back in the water that day and to be honest, I'm still very leery about going into the waves.

But thinking back on that moment, there are a few points I want to magnify that change the whole scary scenario to a really beautiful moment.

I WAS SAFE. All the while the wave was overtaking us, he did not let go of me. He didn't stand beside me holding my hand. HE HELD ME. HE WAS WITH ME. HE PROTECTED ME. Had I been in those rough waters alone, it would have been an emergency situation. When the waters calmed, I WAS STILL IN HIS ARMS. He carried me back to shore and did not put me down until it was safe.

There were many times I disobeyed my parents. I was a feisty child with the heart of a fighter and I got into trouble often. I disappointed them many times. They would scold and punish me because they cared about who I became, but they never stopped loving me. No matter what I did, how bad it was or how disappointed they were about the choice I made, they still loved me. They were always ready and willing to forgive. Because of that, I was free from living in guilt. Once apologies were spoken and reconciliation was made, it was put behind us. I didn't need to keep going back and over it again and again. They didn't remind me of my mess-ups after they were cleared up. It was like they forgot about it. Their compassion motivated me to love and honor them in return.

Just being my birth parents wasn't enough for them. They wanted more than just an identity. They spent time with me and formed a bond, which became a relationship. Because I was a child with a vulnerable heart, I believed the things they said. I trusted them and had faith in them. I depended on them for fulfillment and love. It soon became my lifeline and without it, I would've been an orphan with no life inside of me.

Without God as our Father, and without His love as our lifeline, that is exactly what we are. Orphans with no life inside of us. God's love is meant to be our lifeline. He wants you to live like you are loved. God is to you as a Mother to her newborn child. No matter how painful the labor, once her baby is in her arms, she will never let go. The Mother's love becomes her baby's security.

God is to you as a Father to his small child. His gentle strength carrying his child through the waters and giving him something to lean upon. The Father's strength becomes the child's source of stability.

Let God's love be your security. Let His strength be your stability.

If you want your relationship with Him to flourish, you must receive His love. Fully and completely. In a relationship with a friend or someone you are in love with, think about the difference between being uncertain and doubting that the person loves you, or knowing without a stitch of a question mark that he/she loves you. Without that confidence, you will always be holding back part of your heart because you don't fully trust him/her. You cannot trust someone unless you know for sure they love you. How can you have faith in someone if you doubt their love for you? You won't be able to fully depend on them or believe their promises if you question how they feel about you. This, could be, and is a major cripple in many people's relationship with God. I know it was in mine.

Another dangerous trap is, constantly seeking his approval. When you desperately want someone to like you and you're not sure if they do, you will find yourself "working" to gain affection. You will find ways to manipulate him or impress him to get him to fall in love with you. You so badly want to be accepted, you start to compromise. Changing your standards and pushing convictions aside. You throw away your morals, believing by doing this or that certain thing, you will win his love. When you live like you are loved, and believe that you are loved, your reason for "doing" honorable things in the relationship comes from a completely different drive or source.

The fear of rejection. Just another pothole that is there if you refuse to believe in unconditional love. You cannot go confidently, at peace, resting assured into relation with him, because you are so afraid of being rejected. You keep up all these walls because if he really saw what lies within them he will be disappointed. So you fake it and pretend to be a controlled, got it together kind of person. Being real and vulnerable is too risky. With God, being vulnerable and real is the safest and best way to bring fulfillment into your relationship. And so goes with us humans. If you do not allow yourself to take that risk and "need" that love, you will never be able to fully experience it.

The fear of losing someone. Another big tripper. If you do not fully trust someone and believe in their commitment to you, you fear waking up one day without him in your life. Being obsessed is a very destructive aspect of not living like you are loved. Obsession is what happens when the fear of losing someone controls the way you handle the relationship. You clench tighter and tighter. Grabbing everything you can, forcing your love for her down her throat, and so badly wanting her to return it. Every time you feel unsatisfied, challenged in the relationship or don't get what you think you deserve, you think, "well she must not love me." Obsession is extremely harmful to another's heart. It builds walls, plants fear and closes channels of unconditional, God given love.

So all these different reactions, results and drama. Very applicable to human relationships. These things are happening all around us. Even years after being married.

They are also very applicable to your relationship with God. It could be one, or all of them. Constantly seeking God's approval, and always coming up empty with no stable ground. Fearing rejection, you close your heart to Him. The fear of losing Him or Him leaving you, you become obsessed, trying to control everything around you or trying to control God and tell Him what to do, getting angry when He doesn't respond in the way you would like Him to. An obsessed person is not patient, is not open minded and does not trust.

Now think about being in a relationship with someone, knowing without a doubt that they love you and won't ever leave you. You are fully accepted, and loved unconditionally. The difference here that I'm pointing at is simply this: you, living in doubt of unconditional love and you, living like you are loved with every part of you convinced that you are loved. Believing in that fact brings totally different reaction and results. It takes your relationship to a completely different level and actually creates a totally different relationship. It dramatically changes the way you live in the relationship. Just the fact that he loves you so much, brings you to a place of awe and gratitude. You cannot be thankful for something you don't know you have. Knowing you are deeply loved, gives a stability and creates a confidence to love in return. It gives you a safe place to be vulnerable and open your heart. It motivates you to serve, give, and to honor. Not to "gain" approval or affection, but to return it. Knowing he will never leave you and hanging on to that promise, builds a trust deep within your soul. You are not constantly fearing rejection, or disappointing him, or losing him because you are holding on to the fact that he is extremely committed. The way you know he is committed is because you have experienced and know his heart of love. Being in a relationship with someone that loves you, brings to you life and freedom. Not manipulation or control. You love in return because he has won you over and you want to love him. Not because of a control factor by him. If that's the case, it's not love. Knowing he loves you unconditionally, brings you to a place of approaching the relationship in a completely different way. It impacts who you are and the way you live your life. If you fully believe that you belong to someone, not just by name, title, or identity, but on the heart level, it brings security, belonging, and assurance deep within.

But you have received the spirit of adoption, whereby we cry, "Abba, Father." The Spirit itself bears witness with our spirit, that we are the children of God, and if children, then heirs, (a person who inherits) of God, and joint-heirs with Christ, if so be that we suffer with Him, that we may be also glorified together. Romans 8:15-17

This, is what your Father has in store for you if you believe and comprehend the breadth, length, height, and depth of His love for you. Make it your safe place. Call it your identity. Build every part of your heart and soul upon it. Allow Him to make it your lifeline, your source of life, and your confidence. "Yes, I belong to Him. Yes, I am His child. Yes, He has redeemed me by His blood. Yes, He does love me so much." Allow it to impact and change the way you approach your relationship with Him. Let it be your biggest attraction. Allow it to flow in you and through you, touching everything you do and affecting every heart you are involved in. Come boldly to the throne of His grace, fully dependent on Him, knowing it was Him who formed you in your Mother's womb and believing that YOU ARE LOVED.

Who shall separate us from the love of Christ? Shall tribulation or distress, or persecution, or famine, or nakedness, or peril, or sword? For I am persuaded that neither death, nor life, nor angels, nor principalities, nor powers, nor things present, nor things to come, nor height, nor depth, nor any other creature, shall be able to separate us from the love of God, which is in Christ Jesus our Lord. Romans 8:35-39

6

Relationship: God and You

A relationship means nothing if it is not making a difference in your life. If it's not making a difference in your life, nothing will ever change. If my parents would've been strangers, I wouldn't have called them Mom and Dad. If I wouldn't have had a relationship with them or never would've known them, they would be strangers, regardless of the fact that they're my birth parents. Without knowing them, I wouldn't love them.

You are a perfect creation of the One who loves you more than anyone else ever has or ever will. The Lord's desire is to be connected to you. Like completely and literally connected. No walls, no distance, no hiding in the dark. He knows and understands every piece of your heart and mind. His heart breaks with yours when you are in pain. He rejoices with you in your joy. Because you are His child, He feels everything that you feel. Nothing can separate you from His love. The grace and mercy pouring from His heart will consume you, but only if you want it to and allow Him to work in you and through you.

You wonder why life stays the same and nothing ever changes. It's the same roller coaster of moods, emotions, highs and lows. It's the same dull work day, dragging in and out. The only thing motivating you is the weekend ahead or your next vacation. About when you think you've got it all together, you find yourself messing up again and in a heap.

Do you understand what the depth of a relationship really means? The condition or fact of "being related, connection, association. A connection by blood or marriage." You are already in relation to God. He created you in His image and calls you His child. Before you were even conceived He had dealings with you, because He is the One who had your creation in store. He is the artist of the perfectly done master piece,—you.

So? This does not mean that you are in a relationship with Him or that you have a relationship with Him. "Being related to" and "in relationship with" are two completely different things. There are hundreds of people I'm related to by blood that I've never met. Even if I studied family history, checked out the family tree and learned everything about them, I wouldn't know them if I met them in my backyard.

A relationship with the One who formed you in your Mother's womb goes far beyond just knowing who formed you. It even goes beyond knowing about God and knowing who died and rose again for you. You can have all the spiritual knowledge there is to know, and still be missing the major. To have life brought into your dark world, and to have a stable life of freedom and peace, you need a whole lot more than knowledge about Jesus.

God desires your heart. The heart of something is the central or main part. It is the core. The heart in our bodies is the vital organ to give life to the rest of the body. It is the absolute source of life. It is the root of our existence. When the heart fails, everything fails. When the heart stops pumping, the body stops living.

As I stood in the hospital room by my friend's bedside, I watched him breathe his last breath. The doctors said he was brain dead, therefore the only thing keeping him alive was the breathing machine which kept his heart pumping. Once it was removed, there was nothing to keep life in his heart. I was watching the heart monitor. As his heart slowly gave out, the numbers changed from high to low, then to zero. The lines were moving and jagged, then went straight. His heart stopped pumping air and it was then we knew life had fled.

Just a few short months later, I found myself in the same position. A different hospital, a different friend, but the same pain and the same agony. The night she passed into eternity, her room was filled with people, so I stood outside. There were monitors and screens outside the room, and again, I was watching them. When the heart rate hit zero and the line went straight, I knew she was gone.

The heart is the source of life in the physical body. It is also the core of everything else about you. Heartbreak, heartaches, lighthearted, and many more terms with the word "heart" in them are used to express what we feel inside. When we connect with someone or something, our heart is the core of that connection. When you hear the term "it pulled at my heartstrings" it means they were emotionally attached to a situation or person.

Your spiritual or emotional heart, which is very connected to your soul, is the core of you as a person. It is the central and main part of you. It is your source of life. Everything that you do and say is a result of what is lying within your heart.

Again I say, "God desires your heart." Your core. Your vital organ. He doesn't just want the outer-layer or shell of your inner self, but the core of it. The root. The source of your life. He wants to dwell in your heart, hold your heart, protect your heart, and through that, connect to everything that your heart is connected to. The root, the source of your life, He longs to saturate it and flow out of it and onto everything that you touch.

There's gotta be at least one person you really care about that you have a relationship with. How did you get there? What do you do to keep the relationship going? Most likely if your friend is important to you, you'll spend time together. You'll take time out of your busy schedule to catch up. You will want to know more about him than where he lives and where he works. Your relationship will go way beyond just knowledge about each other. You will search each other's hearts. And when you do come to that point of really knowing each other and being attached, are you like, "ok, since we know each other good enough, there's no need to keep in touch?" Probably not. If you're wired like the rest of us humans, you will want to stay connected or become even more connected. Your heart is now involved. If time goes by without a recent chat or heart to heart, you will notice the absence. It will create a void. Distance.

God doesn't do void. Distance is not on His agenda. He desires your heart, attention and your passion. All of it. **Psalm 63 David wrote with fervent passion. "Oh God, Thou art my God. Early will I seek Thee. My soul thirsteth for Thee. My flesh longs for Thee in a dry and thirsty land, where no water is. To see Thy power and Thy glory, so as I have seen Thee in the sanctuary. Because Thy lovingkindess is BETTER THAN LIFE, my lips shall praise Thee. Thus will I bless Thee while I live, I will lift up my hands in your name. My soul shall be satisfied as with marrow and fatness, and my mouth shall praise Thee with joyful lips. When I remember Thee upon my bed, and meditate upon Thee in the night watches. Because Thou hast been my help, therefore in the shadow of Thy wings will I rejoice. MY SOUL FOLLOWETH HARD AFTER THEE, Thy right Hand upholdeth me."**

I am seeing a relationship that is "better than life." Better than life!!! That's deep. That's real. It's crazy and radical. That's exactly what God wants for us. A relationship with Him that is better than the best things in life. He wants to be your biggest dream, your highest hope, and your ALL in all. He made your soul to "follow hard after Him." He longs to have you seek Him "firmly and unyieldingly."

Are you calling Christ your "Father" or your "God," when you don't even know Him? Do you think you know Him if you're not in a relationship with Him? How can you possibly fall in love with Him if you don't spend time with Him and seek a deeper relationship with Him?

By responding to God's never-changing love and mercy, change is unavoidable. You will begin to want more of Him and you will find yourself falling in love with Him.

When we fall in love with someone or really want to connect with someone, our desires suddenly have a lot to do with what the other wants. We start liking things we didn't even know we did, simply because being in a relationship with them exposed our heart to something of the other's interests.

As you fall in love with and become more connected to God, His interests become exciting to you. You will wonder what it is He wants you to do with the life He has given you. His desires become your desires.

God wants you to tell Him your deepest struggles and shame. He already knows all about it, but He wants to get in there with you and heal those areas. It is Satan that wants to keep it hidden and out of sight. It is him that makes the shame too great to bring it out. Because he knows once a wound is exposed is when the Healer can do His miracle upon that wound and as long as he can get you to keep it locked away, it will never be healed. Evil despises healing. God invests in healing. God can't help you if you don't open those doors and ask Him to tear down those walls.

If you have children, do you want your child to wait to tell you about a problem until after it's figured out or after he's been dealing with it for years? If your child would be involved in pornography, alcohol, drugs or anything else destructive and you wouldn't know about it, but you could help him if you would know about it, would you want him to keep it hidden from you? Needing your help but too ashamed or too proud to admit it, creating a wall of separation. Or would you want him to come to you with an open heart, needing your strength and guidance?

So often guilt and shame or pride and haughtiness keep us from coming to God with an open heart, robbing us and stripping us from the very thing He wants for us. A relationship with Him.

The enemy uses many different lies to brainwash our minds. "You're an idiot. You're not worthy. Look at what you did. He will never forgive you or even care about you because you're too pathetic. You'll be right back anyway. Give it up. You don't deserve it." Now on the flip side he speaks more lies but quite differently. "You don't need anyone. Asking for help is wimpy. You're a weakling. Toughen up. You don't need to be saved by someone. You're a good person. You'll go to heaven. You deserve it. All the bad stuff in your life is everyone else's fault. Look how good you are. Everyone likes you. You don't need help. You've got it all under control."

He speaks lies of condemnation, lies of flattery, lies of self-righteousness and many more. Believing those lies bring forth results of self-condemnation or pride. Either one is not from God. Self-condemnation holds us in bondage of guilt and shame, pride holds us in bondage of never needing a Savior, or bondage of bringing glory to ourselves when it all belongs to God. Satan uses them to keep us away from God and away from the truth. They are lies and as long as we believe them, and don't know the real truth about ourselves, there will be a wall between us and God.

The truth is, we are sinners, in total need of a Savior. But God loves us so much. Yes, so much, He died for us. He dealt with our condemnation on the cross. He bore the shame, endured the pain and He died a gruesome death to save our pitiful souls.

As I gaze at the cross and see the blood running off of His body and onto the dirt beneath Him, every drop is filled with grace. Standing there helpless, at a loss of knowing what I can do to help with my salvation, I watch as my condemnation is nailed to the cross. As I witness the grace filled blood continue to flow, working out my salvation, I realize, I did nothing to earn the grace that is so freely falling from Himself. At the same time I also realize, I need it desperately. Without it I will die.

I see the outstretched arms, torn and bleeding, and the hole gaping in His side. There is only One who is dying for the world that day. And that's when I also see my pride being nailed to the cross, the blood washing all over it. For I now see, it is Him who saved me. I am still standing there and watching, doing nothing to participate. Only needing His grace. Always needing His grace.

Because we have problems, we need a Problemsolver. Because we are sick, we need a Healer. Because we are weak in the midst of the storm, we need a Solid Rock to stand on. Because we are guilty, ashamed, unworthy and dirty, we need Jesus' blood applied to all that muck to flip it all around.

So in your guilt, shame, sin, or pride, come to Him. **He says, "come to Me, all you who are heavyladen, (very tired, troubled, and burdened) and I will give you rest."** He didn't say, "oh my goodness, you are a complete mess! Get it together already and clean yourself up, then come to me." No, He is saying, "come with your sin and your shame. Come with whatever baggage you are carrying, because I am the only One who can take it for you and give you rest."

As long as you keep hiding behind those walls, too guilty to show your face or too proud to admit you need help, you will continue to be miserable.

Just as you care about the struggles in your child's life, so the Father cares about yours and even way beyond your imagination. Nothing is too small or too far beneath God for Him to care about. From the broken toe to the disease eating away your body, the empty bank account to what you did on Friday night. He knows, He cares. The details in your life are never a burden to Him. He delights in your confiding in Him and has a mega passion for healing and restoring your broken pieces.

Let not your sin and your shame, or your pride and haughtiness keep you away from the One who loves you. Let it drive you to the cross, in need of the grace filled blood made available, so you could have abundant life in Him forever.

7

God Doesn't Do Dead Ends

Jesus did not come to destroy us, but to save us. Luke 9:56 The angel of the Lord encamps round about them that fear Him, and delivers them. Psalm 34:7 He is nigh unto them that are of a broken heart, and saves such as be of a contrite spirit. Many are the afflictions of the righteous, but the Lord delivers him out of all. Psalm 34:18-19

He will deliver me out of ALL??? Not just some, or even most of my afflictions, but all?! Every teeny tiny pain to the most enormous monsters in my life, He will deliver me. He will bring you through and carry you, not only through, but out of them. He will set you free from every bondage, release you and save you. He will restore every pain, every wound, and fill dark despair with His light of hope. He will bring a new day upon you, a new sunrise, a new beginning, a new birth. He will bring you to a place where you can fully believe He has removed your transgressions as far as the east is from the west. He will carry out and do as He has promised. This is what it means to be delivered. Radical, assuring and stedfast promises. That's our God.

So why the trials, heartbreaks, disappointments, ruined plans, broken dreams, and shattered hopes? Does God love me so much and want me to desire and need Him so much that He allows these things? The challenges, turmoil, hurts, and impossible days? It doesn't really make sense, but think about it. Of course you wouldn't want your own child or someone you love, be in pain, especially if you would have every power to remove it. So really, that must be hard for God to allow us to walk through some of this stuff, when He, in the blink of an eye, could remove it all.

At one time I thought maybe painful situations are a punishment of some sort. I know some of the hardest times in my journey were consequences of my own sin, and me making bad decisions and following after what I wanted, not being patient enough to listen to the voice of God and forgetting to put Him first and foremost. We do suffer because of bad decisions and sin has consequences. It always has, and it will continue to have, as long as the earth is standing.

But what about the things that simply crush your spirit? The things that break your heart and make you weak and broken? The times you find yourself stripped of everything else. When your world is wrecked and falling apart. Your mind is numb and you're in a fog that doesn't seem to lift. Why does God allow these things?

Believing and praying your best friend, your son, your brother, your dad, your husband would heal. Every piece of hope you had, shattered. Looking upon his face in a casket, trying to find a way to breathe through the crushing pain. Someone you love has left the earth, leaving you to live without him. Facing the cold, hard grip of death, you can't get away. You want to wake up from the nightmare, but it just continues, leaving you drained, not knowing who you are anymore and wondering how in the world life will ever be liveable again.

Your mother, your wife, best friend, sister, aunt, daughter, gone in the blink of an eye. In a heavy fog, you watch as the hearse takes her to her place of burial. You want to run to escape the pain, but you can't. You're engulfed with waves of sadness unlike anything you ever knew was even possible, as you stand by her grave, watching with dread, the unbelievable.

Watching someone you love, make all the wrong decisions. Seeing her miserable in her addictions, you're at a loss of what to do because you have no control. As you watch her fall deeper and deeper, your heart is being crushed. She is your daughter you carried for nine months. She is your best friend that you don't even know anymore. Your once innocent sister you spent hours with in the same home. You pray, you weep for her, longing for her to return. Knowing she needs more. Knowing she IS more.

The manipulating and controlling boyfriend who condemns you when you make the decision to leave the relationship. You thought you loved him, but realized you didn't and don't know what to do, but leave. The wrath and guilt he puts upon you causing you deep pain, and agonizing fear, bringing you to a place so low, and not knowing how to rise out of it and move forward.

Someone you loved for a long time, finally came into your life. Making promises, pursuing and begging your heart, affection, and love. Persuaded, you think you're destined to be together, so you give. Body, emotions and soul. Then comes the day of it not working out. The time of knowing you must let go, but having no idea how. You have built your life around this person and everything you dreamt of, hoped upon, and believed in, is now in pieces. Your heart is shattered and you don't even know where to begin picking up the pieces.

The people that have rejected you, the parents that never loved you. The way you've been used and abused. The gutwrenching pain, disappointments, and failures. The choices that bring shattered hearts, and broken worlds. The sleepless nights bringing you to complete exhaustion. Crushed, pushed to the ground, flat on your face. No strength left to get up or even try to look up. Motivation? Gone. Courage? Vanished. Trust? No idea where to find it. You once felt invincible. Now you feel defeated and hopeless in the midst of your grief. Feeling suffocated with pain, you don't know which way to go. Everything blurs together. Nothing to do but cry more tears and feel more hurt.

Why does God allow us to come to these places? The places we would change in a minute if we could. I cannot answer that question, but I have discovered that He will go to that extent of painful love, to get my eyes on Him. He knows how much I desperately need Him and how quickly I forget that I do. He wants you to abide in Him and Him only.

"No other gods before Me. I have chosen you. Abide in Me and I will abide in you," are only a few of the many things He speaks of in His word about a one on one relationship with Him. Intimate and all the way. Him and you. That's what He wants.

I know He has a reason for everything He allows into your life, and yes, many of those things are a result of the evil around us and are not what He wants for you, but He will use them for His glory and your good if you TRUST HIM. No matter how bad it is, encountered by Jesus, miracles flow forth. God will allow valleys of darkness and deserts of dry, hot sand in your life, but He will never leave you. That alone is a miracle. HE WILL NEVER LEAVE YOUR SIDE. When you are broken, with nothing left to give. When you are dry, barren, and numb, wondering, "how can I stand up when I have nothing?" It is in those moments another miracle takes place. Because you are empty, God can fill that place. Because your life is falling apart and everything is out of control, God takes control and holds the pieces in the palm of His Hand. It is then you experience none other than the heart of God Almighty Himself, picking you up, giving you words to speak, oxygen to breathe, and strength to put one foot in front of the other. He portrays His glory in ways we would never think of. In those darkest times of pain are the times He uses His strength to draw us closer to Him. When we are weak, then He is strong.

In 2 Corinth. 12, Paul speaks the words Jesus said to him after he was asking Him to remove the thorn in his flesh. And He said unto me, "My grace is sufficient for thee: FOR MY STRENGTH IS MADE PEREFCT IN WEAKNESS." Then Paul goes on to tell the people this, "most gladly therefore

will I rather glory in my infirmities THAT THE POWER OF CHRIST MAY REST UPON ME. Therefore I take pleasure in infirmities, (physical weakness or ailment, lack of strength,) in reproaches, (objects of scorn or contempt, blame, disgrace, or discredit) in necessities, in persecutions, in distresses for Christ's sake: FOR WHEN I AM WEAK, THEN I AM STRONG."

Paul took pleasure in hard times, because that's when he got through, only by the power of God on him, in him, and through him. He loved experiencing that power and God's miracles in his valleys. He got by the best when he needed God the most.

God is a miracle-worker. He works in the midst of the valleys in ways that bring us to complete awe and amazement of Him. He works things out in our lives in ways that we could never give ourselves an ounce of credit. If something happens in your life that could've been done by you or someone else, it's not a miracle. Some things that we see as small and insignificant, are actually miracles straight from the Hand of God. Take the breath of life and try to put it there yourself, you can't. Make the sun come up new even just one time. You won't come close. There are many miracles we miss every day because we are too busy or too distracted.

A miracle that brings me to complete awe is, the miracle of Him never leaving our side. The King of kings, the Lord of lords, the Holy One, feels your pain. He is not just watching over you, observing everything you deal with, HE IS RIGHT THERE IN THE MIDST OF IT. HE IS WITH YOU. ALL THE WAY. Yes all the way. Sometimes it doesn't feel that way and you really just don't sense His presence at all. Then there are other times when you could wrap yourself in Him being so near. The times you don't "feel" Him near, you must believe He is, because He promises He is. Draw near to Him, cry out to Him, believing and expecting that He is with you. Sometimes our pain blocks out the feeling of His presence and it is then you must hang on, with all your grip, to the "knowing" that He is near. Be faithful in your pain. He will come through. Another miracle is this, God never breaks His promises. Good or evil. He will do as He speaks.

Isaiah 41, God says, "fear not, for I am with thee. Be not dismayed, for I am thy God. I will strengthen thee. Yes, I will uphold thee with the right hand of my righteousness."

Isaiah 43, But now says the Lord that created thee, "oh Jacob," and He that formed thee, "oh Israel, fear not. For I have redeemed thee. I have called thee by thy name. Thou art mine. When you pass through the waters, I will be with you, and through the rivers, they will not overflow you, when you walk through the fire, you will not be burned, neither shall the flame kindle upon you. For I am the Lord your God, the Holy One of Israel, your Savior."

God doesn't do dead ends. He does not quit on you in the valley, nor does He stop when He has carried you through. He brings you to a new place. He will transform all your areas of hurt and bring His power and glory into the place and do His work for good. No, He never stops at a hard place.

Isaiah 54, "Oh thou afflicted, tossed with tempest and not comforted, behold, I will lay thy stones with colorful gems, and lay thy foundations with sapphires. And I will make thy windows of agates, and thy gates of sparkling jewels, and all thy borders of pleasant stone."

Isaiah 41, "When the poor and needy seek water and there is none, and their tongue faileth for thirst, I, the God of Israel, will not forsake them. I will open rivers in high places, and FOUNTAINS IN THE MIDST OF THE VALLEYS, I will make the WILDERNESS A POOL OF WATER, AND THE DRY LAND, SPRINGS OF WATER."

God didn't change. The God of Israel, is the God of the world. The God of Jacob, Is the God of you. Take these scriptures personally. They were recorded and written to last forever for every single soul that ever was, and is, and is to come. There are many more scriptures of promise in the Word. If you do not fully believe them, you are

47

underestimating God and dwindling on faith. The darkness is never victorious.

Think about the sunrise. God is so faithful. Every single day, right on time, the sun rises. Sometimes it's hidden by clouds, but it's rising just the same. Day breaks and all is new again. There is never a night without a sunrise somewhere. If you live in an area where the sun doesn't come out for a season, it returns at the right time. God never fails.

And so He is with life. Your pain is not the winner, nor is it victorious. Not with God involved. With Jesus involved, He is the winner. The good overcomes the bad. God is the glorified One. The light is always more powerful than the dark. It can be the blackest night, no stars or moon, and once those rays of the sun hit earth, which one is more noticed, magnified and powerful? The black of the night, or the rays of the sun? With God in your mess, evil, death, pain, sorrow, grief, or any other crazy hard thing is never the winner. It is not the conqueror. The rays of Christ fade away the night of your pain and He becomes the victorious One.

Pain lasts a long time, and years after a situation occurs, it can still hurt. But if it is still "controlling" you, affecting the way you live, bringing negative results or destructive manner, it is because you have chosen to wallow in it. You have allowed it to become a stronghold. Bitterness, anger, hatred to oneself, others, or God, are only a few results of "choosing to stay in the valley." God won't heal those wounds if you don't allow Him to get very personal with those wounds. He won't bring you out of the valley and into the fountains if you don't allow Him to get into the grittiest part of the valley with you. He won't turn your rocks into colorful gems if you refuse to give Him your rocks. You will never see your mess turn into a miracle until you invite Him into the mess. If you choose to stay in a dark cellar, you will miss His glorious sunrise.

Psalm 91, "he that dwelleth in the secret place of the Most High, shall abide under the shadow of the Almighty. Surely He shall deliver thee from the snare of the fowler, (bird-

hunter) and from the noisome pestilence, (harmful disease, plague, anything evil) He shall cover thee with His feathers, and under His wings shalt thou trust. His truth shall be thy shield and buckler." He says to you in verses 14–16, "because he has set his love upon Me, therefore will I deliver him, I will set him on high, (protect him) because he hath known My name. He shall call upon Me and I will answer him. I will be with him in trouble. I will deliver him and honor him. With long life will I satisfy him and show him My Salvation."

No matter how long and dark the tunnel, how low the valley, how evil your surroundings, how torn up your emotions and wellbeing, how broken your heart, pathetic the situation, long for Him. Set your love upon Him and He will deliver you. Know His name and He will answer you. Patiently wait on Him and believe in something Higher than the situation you're in right now. He never asks us to go alone. He carries us. He covers you with His feathers and hides you with His wings. He honors you. He will satisfy you and reveal to you His perfect and complete salvation.

Isaiah 45 holds this promise, "I will go before you and make the crooked places straight. I will break in pieces the gates of brass, and cut through the bars of iron. I will give you the treasures of darkness, and hidden riches of secret places, that you may know that I the Lord, which calls you by your name, am the God of Israel."

Invite Him into your crooked places. Give Him your gates of brass and bars of iron. He will not bring you to a dead end. He will carry you over into the sunrise and delight in pouring His glorious rays onto your darkest night.

Oh taste, and see that the Lord is good. Psalm 34

8

Rejoicing During Affliction

The multitude rose up together against Paul and Silas, and the magistrates tore off their clothes, and commanded to beat them. And when they had laid many stripes upon them they cast them into prison, charging the jailer to keep them safely: the jailer thrust them into the inner prison, and made their feet fast in the stocks. And at midnight Paul and Silas prayed, and sang praises unto God: and the prisoners heard them. And suddenly there was a great earthquake, so that the foundations of the prison were shaken: and immediately all the doors were opened, and everyone's bands were loosed. Acts 16:22-26

It was a rough night. They were doing what God was calling them to do and suffering for it. Do you think they understood? Did it make sense to them? They probably questioned and wondered, "where was God now?" But they didn't stop praising Him. Their voices rang through the prison cells that night, echoing through the halls. It wasn't murmering and complaining, swearing or cursing. It was all out praise and worship. Crying out to the One who redeemed their souls. Those around them heard it. And then all went wild. God was there. He chose a perfect time to come through and reveal His power. Had the keeper of the prison not saw and experienced what he did, he would've not done what he did next.

Trembling, he fell down before Paul and Silas. He asked what he must do to be saved. Paul and Silas told him to believe on the Lord Jesus Christ and spoke to him and to all that were in his house the Word of the Lord. He then took them, and washed their stripes and was baptized. He brought them to his house and fed them. He rejoiced, believing in God, with all his house.

In time of affliction, rejoicing brings breakthrough. As those around you witness you being bound and crying out to Him, they will stand in awe with you as the chains break loose. Your hard times and overcoming them, is a testimony of God's power to those around you.

While reading through Isaiah, I was taught so many new things. God revealed to me truths, promises and hope in the words. One of the deepest was how much He really does love me and wants what He knows is best for me. And no matter how bad the situation, how deep the pain and affliction, He never stops there. He always brings water into that desert. In Christ there is always victory, never defeat. God is a God of winning, conquering, of raising up and bringing new life into the places that were dead. Sometimes it takes a long time and the desert seems endless. It just doesn't work how our flesh so often wishes it would. We would prefer a really small desert where we can see the river ahead, soon get to that river, and then take a nice long vacation there. It just doesn't work that way. Healing from major pain often takes a really long time. It is a process.

And the question is, "what do we do in that period of time?"

In the previous chapter it's all about us completely needing God, holding on to Him and Him being faithful in your darkest night. Surrendering, allowing yourself to be broken and needy of Him. You being protected by Him and covered in His strength. Yes, that is a major.

In those times of my life, I could not deal with the pain, or even get up in the morning without my Father's strength flowing through

51

me. Many times, I didn't even realize how involved He actually was, but looking back now, I know there is no way I could've gotten through and came out ok, without Him carrying me.

There is another major in time of trial. Actually a double major. I asked the question, "what do we do in this period of processing pain, or walking through a fire?"

Read Isaiah 51:6 with me and allow the perfect truth to sink in. Our God said, "lift up your eyes to the heavens, and look upon the earth beneath; for the heavens shall vanish away like smoke. And the earth shall grow old like a garment, and they that dwell therein shall die in like manner; BUT MY SALVATION SHALL BE FOREVER, AND MY RIGHTEOUSNESS SHALL NOT BE PUT TO AN END."

The answer to the question is not in the verse, but the REASON for the answer to the question is written all over.

What do you do in a hard time? You want to be victorious, an overcomer, and attain joy? The answer is simple. Be thankful. "Wait a minute," you're thinking. "How can I be thankful when my whole life is falling apart? There is no way I can be thankful right now." Many of us don't wanna hear that one. I know I didn't. What reason is there to be thankful? Read the scripture again. **HIS SALVATION SHALL BE FOREVER. THOUGH EVERYTHING FALLS APART AND DIES, HIS RIGHTEOUSNESS WILL NEVER BE REMOVED.**

That is a promise my friend. That is the number one reason to be thankful in a hard time. No matter what gets taken away, salvation and eternal life in Jesus gives us reason to be overflowing with gratitude to the One who redeems us and calls us His own. No matter how deep your grief is, it cannot take away your salvation unless you yourself make that choice.

As I was wallowing in pain, I was fighting my way through, trying to find some kind of something that makes sense. I was being attacked spiritually, emotionally, and physically. There was a lot of turmoil going on that I didn't know what to do with.

For some reason, when we are having a hard time is when the enemy really starts pressing in. During a rough time, we are extra vulnerable and weak and Satan sees those open doors and will take advantage of those open doors. What can simply be a time of grief can turn into a real battlefield of good and evil, if we are unaware of the enemy's attack. Depression, stress, anxiety, fatigue, and everything else tied into that realm, are emotions we deal with when under attack. God uses hard times to portray His power, and to do His perfect molding in our hearts. He uses them to pull us towards Him and make Himself very real to us. Satan uses them to bring us to a low so low, we lose the desire to live. God delights in life, Satan delights in death. Not only physically, but also emotionally and spiritually. He wants to kill your soul, spirit, mind, and then when he has those dead, he wants your body also. Many times when we are sick emotionally and spiritually, our physical body starts reacting. The three are very connected. God wants to bring abundant life to your soul, spirit and mind. And when He brings those to life, your physical body will have incredible results. Yes, we are on a battlefield every single day. Our souls are being fought for, by One who loves us and one who wants to destroy us. Whose side are we on?

As I was being attacked, I knew it and I felt it. Therefore I fought it. I fought it by coming to God and rebuking evil in His name. I cried out to God to win the battle and bring freedom from this pit I was in. I kept fighting and I kept being attacked.

One evening, a dear friend of mine and I went to Panera Bread to catch up. I shared about what was going on. She spoke to me about rejoicing. I was like, "what???" Rejoicing? I had never really thought about it during this time. I mean everything seemed so ridiculous, what was there to rejoice about? Yeah sure, rejoice when things are good, but when I can't think anything but the low I'm in, rejoice? But how?

She spoke life-changing words that night. This is what she said. "If you want a real tool against Satan, be thankful. Praise the Lord. Rejoice in Him FOR SALVATION and FOR BEING WITH YOU

THROUGH THIS TRIAL. That gives you so much power against him. Find things to be thankful about."

I'll never forget it. It was a moment of a major switch in my spiritual life. It became my new perspective, my new prayer, and my new cry.

"Lord, thank you. For being with me through this trial. For walking with me through this valley. For abiding with me and being here in this time of pain. I rejoice in Your name, for You are Sovereign, Holy, Righteous, and Almighty, Loving and All-powerful. Everything that comes my way, every trial, every heartache, is controlled by You. You have filtered these trials, therefore You are the Winner. You are victorious in my life because You are in control of all the "stuff" that comes my way. Wickedness has no power because You are my God, my Rock, my Mighty Fortress. Evil and hell are way beneath You. No matter what I'm going through, I am safe, I am protected, and best of all, I am Yours."

I wrote this prayer down and stuck it on my mirror. I read it continuously. I thanked Him for His love and salvation continuously. It was breakthrough. It was like a complete turnaround. No, it didn't all happen in one night where suddenly I was walking on water, free of hurt. It started slowly. Little by little. I found reason to live again. Joy started creeping in on me again. As the light started saturating my soul, the darkness began to fade away. As I reached up to the heavens with a grateful heart to the One who saved me and walks with me, He reached down and filled my life with blessing and abundance, healing and miracles in ways I never thought possible.

No matter where you are, what you are dealing with, rejoice. Rejoice. Rejoice. Number one reason, HIS SALVATION IS FOREVER. Number two, HE IS WITH YOU. Number three, YOU ARE HIS. Number 4,5,6, and on and on . . . fill in the blanks. It's your call. Find things to be thankful for. Find something to rejoice about. Even if it's something small, it's powerful in the name of Jesus.

Art Thou not it which hath dried the sea, the waters of the great deep, That hath made the depths of the sea a way for the

ransomed to pass over? **Therefore the redeemed of the Lord shall return and come with singing unto Zion, and everlasting joy shall be upon their head, they shall obtain gladness and joy. Sorrow and mourning shall flee away. I, EVEN I, AM HE THAT COMFORTETH YOU. BUT I AM THE LORD THY GOD, THAT DIVIDED THE SEA, WHOSE WAVES ROARED, The Lord of hosts is His name. Isaiah 51:10-15**

Consider the children of Israel. Their enemy was coming up behind them and they had no way out for they were facing an ocean. A huge, roaring ocean. They looked like the losers. Oh, but God was on their side. He did the impossible. He parted the waters and made a way.

Face your ocean with God on your side, fighting for you. He is doing the impossible. He is making a way. Praise Him.

9

Victory over Death

He (Jesus) is despised and rejected of men, a man of sorrows, and acquainted with grief, and we hid as if it were our faces from Him. He was despised and we esteemed Him not. Surely He hath borne our griefs and carried our sorrows, yet we did esteem Him stricken, smitten of God, and afflicted. BUT HE WAS WOUNDED FOR OUR TRANSGRESSIONS, HE WAS BRUISED FOR OUR INIQUITIES, THE CHASTISEMENT OF OUR PEACE WAS UPON HIM, AND WITH HIS STRIPES WE ARE HEALED. Isaiah 53:3-5

Jesus' life on earth must've been a long continuous stretch of trial. He left all of heaven's glory and His Father's presence and came to earth, which in comparison to heaven, where do I start? The earth is beautiful, but anyone that has a vision of heaven, does not want to come back. Jesus coming to earth was maybe a little like me living in our cellar for 30 years. And probably worse. He left the warmth, the perfection and the safety of God, and was put into the womb of a human being as a helpless little child. He then endured being born. Yes, that is painful for a baby. Especially when going from 98.6 degrees to a cold stable. He was born in the midst of animals and the smell of them. The stable was no mansion, nor a place fit for a King. It was more like a cave in the side of a hill. One of the lowliest places that existed. Many of us, as humans, wouldn't even consider spending a night in a stable if we could at all prevent it. This was a King. One of royalty. He deserved the finest, richest bed and blankets, but His bed was a manger. He went from being a heavenly, spiritual being, to a human being. He now had every nerve and feeling humans have. He was God in flesh. He experienced pain, discomfort, and tears. And He was also tempted just as we are.

Now moving ahead to the night He died. Death. The cold, harsh word. He came to earth to die the most torturous death. And He did nothing to deserve one scratch on His body. Yet, here He was. Knowing exactly what was ahead. He told His disciples of it. **(Mark 9:30)** He knew pure and unrelenting torture was coming, and He was dreading it.

Matthew 26,27,28, Mark 14,15,16, and Luke 22,23,24 speak of Jesus' death and resurrection. The reason He came.

On that night, Jesus was sorrowful and very heavy. He fell on His face, crying out to God in His grief, "Abba, Father, all things are possible unto Thee. Let this cup pass from me." Yet, He said, "not as I will, but as Thou wilt." An angel appeared unto Him from heaven, strengthening Him. Being in agony, He prayed more earnestly, His sweat like great drops of blood falling to the ground beneath Him. He was coming to His Father on the worst night of His life, seeking deliverance, but very surrendered. When He returned to His disciples, He found them sleeping. On the craziest, most overwhelming night of His life, His best friends were crashing out on Him. He left them sleep, and returned to pray to His Father, saying the same words. When His disciples didn't get it, God did. Jesus sought His ultimate fulfillment in God. Nobody else understood that night.

When He returned to His disciples, He told them, "rise, let us be going, behold he is at hand that doeth betray me." In a moment, while He was still speaking, Judas, His follower, a servant of His, betrayed Him. He gave his Master to the enemy. He called Him,

"Master" and kissed Him. Jesus then said, "friend, for what cause have you come?" Notice He called him "friend." His very own friend betrayed Him that night and gave Him to the enemy in exchange for money.

That same hour, the disciples forsook Him and fled. Come on! When he needed supporters the most, there were none to be found. In the most necessary moment for His friends to be there for Him, they decided to skip out. They were afraid of what was happening. They didn't slowly fade away in the background, or get lost in the crowd. They intentionally ran away, fast.

From a distance, Peter followed Him to the high priest's palace to see the outcome. He sat in with the servants and warmed himself by the fire. He did not go in and defend Jesus. He did not take a stand for his soul mate. He denied him. Flat out, three times. At their last meal together, they had a conversation. The Lord said, "Simon, Satan hath desired to have you, that he may sift you as wheat: but I have prayed for thee, that thy faith fail not: and when you have returned to me, strengthen thy brethren." Peter replies, "Lord, I am ready to go with thee, both into prison and into death." Jesus said, "before the cock crows twice, you will deny me three times." Peter spoke more vehemently, (strongly emotional, intense, passionate, marked by great energy) "if I should die with Thee, I will not deny Thee in any wise." All them that were with Him, also said likewise. When the time came, Peter refused knowing Him. He cursed and swore he didn't know his best friend, his lifeline, his Master. While he was denying Him the third time, the cock crew. Jesus turned and looked upon Peter. As Jesus was looking, the cock was crowing and Peter remembered their conversation. He went out and wept bitterly.

As Jesus was accused, blindfolded, spit on, struck and slapped, he did nothing to try to defend Himself. He didn't yell, curse, or make a scene that night. He was submitted to His Father's purpose for His life. He took a stand and spoke the truth. When they asked Him, "are you the Christ, the Son of the Blessed?" He replied, "I am; and you shall see the Son of man sitting on the right hand of power, and coming in the clouds of heaven." He knew it would make them furious, but He spoke the truth in a strong, profound way, without trying to prove His point or throwing His opinion in arrogance.

In the morning, they took counsel against Jesus to put Him to death. They bound Him, took Him away, and delivered Him to Pontius Pilot. The people then chose to bring back to town, Barabbas. A sick murderer. They preferred having him on the streets over Jesus, the One of Love. They wanted Him dead. Crucified and done with. So Pilate gave in to the pressure of the people. Peer pressure. He knew something wasn't right. He even washed his hands in front of the people saying, "I am innocent of the blood of this just person." He then had Him scourged and delivered Him to be crucified.

Judas, when he saw what was happening, repented himself, and brought the money to the chief priests and elders, saying, "I have sinned in that I have betrayed the innocent blood." And they said, "what is that to us? See to that yourself." Judas threw the money down in the temple, departed, and went and hung himself.

Then the soldiers took Jesus into the common hall, and gathered unto Him the whole band of soldiers. They stripped Him and put on Him a scarlet robe. They twisted a crown of thorns and put it on His head. They put a reed in His right hand and bowed their knees before Him, mocking Him. They spit on Him, took the reed and smote Him on the head. They took the scarlet robe off of him and put His own raiment on Him, then led Him away to crucify Him.

He was at a loss of sleep, probably hadn't eaten or drank anything for a while. He was beaten, torn, and bleeding, barely recognizable, if at all. And the worst was yet to come. The road ahead looked dark and impossible. They came to Golgotha and gave Him vinegar mixed with gall to drink. He tasted and then refused it.

They crucified Him. The spikes ripping into the flesh, the nerves, and the bones of His hands and His feet. He felt every bit of it. He was not unconscious. There was no morphine, laughing gas, anesthesia, advil, or whiskey. Nothing to relieve the pain.

They parted His garments and gambled for them. They sat down and watched Him suffer. There, covered in all the filth, muck, and grime of the sins of the world, He hung. Covered and dripping in the stench of it. He was bearing it all. All the wrong ever done, from the teeniest white lie to the worst massacre ever, He suffered for it. He died for it. For three hours He hung in darkness, and then cried out, "My God, My God, why have You forsaken me?" He then cried again with a loud voice and yielded up the ghost. All life was gone. He was defeated. It looked like a hopeless case.

The disciple's life purpose was gone. The Son Mary loved, held, cuddled and raised, dead on a cross.

The veil of the temple was ripped in two, from the top to the bottom. Read about the curtain in **Exodus 26:31–32**. This curtain was no small deal. It's amazing. The earth quaked, the rocks split, the graves were opened and many bodies of the saints which slept, arose. The people feared greatly, saying, "truly this was the Son of God."

The night that changed the way everything was. It was turmoil, confusion, and nothing made sense. It was radical and nobody understood.

But there was One who did. He had orchestrated every stitch of it. There was a perfect and very necessary work being taken place in His Son. What had been prophesied was being brought forth because there was One who was extremely committed and surrendered to His Father.

In the evening, Jesus' body was brought down off the cross, wrapped in a clean linen cloth and laid in a new tomb. The tomb had been hewn out of a rock. A great stone was rolled to the door of the tomb. Sitting against the sepulcher were the women who followed Jesus and loved Him. They must've been heartbroken. The Love of their life was gone.

The chief priests and Pharisees remembered Jesus' words of rising in three days. They called Him a deceiver and were afraid the disciples would come and take His body in the night, so they secured the tomb, sealed the stone and set a watch.

It seemed over and done with. Evil conquered, hope was gone, defeat in control. But it wasn't. Not even close.

Go forward to the dawning of the day after Sabbath, and as the sun rises, you are on the brink of victory. Walk with the two Mary's as they go to the grave to grieve. Take a step closer to the grave where Jesus lay dead, and witness the most chilling, glorious place of victory, ever.

There was another earthquake. The angel of the Lord descended from heaven, came, and rolled back the stone of the door and sat upon it. His face was like lightning, and his raiment was white as snow. The men keeping watch, shook, and became as dead men. They literally passed out.

Listen intently as the angel speaks the beautiful words of promise and hope. "Fear not. For I know you seek Jesus, which was crucified. He is not here. He is risen, as He said. Come, see the place where the Lord lay. Go quickly and tell His disciples He is risen from the dead. And behold, He goeth before you into Galilee. There you shall see Him."

They departed with fear and great joy, and ran to bring His disciples word. As they went to tell His disciples, behold, Jesus met them, saying, "All hail." They came and held Him by the feet and worshipped Him. The eleven disciples went away into Galilee where Jesus had appointed them, and when they saw Him, they worshipped Him.

LIFE. Pure, sweet life. So new, so refreshing and so incredible. Life forever. Life more powerful than death. Life undefeated.

Death was not the end of the story. The stench, the blood, the pain and grit of it, now gone forever. Almighty God was working His perfect miracle in an extremely hard situation. Jesus was completely trusting His Father and knew He wouldn't leave Him in the grave. Had it stopped there, God would've never brought Jesus to that place.

Whatever God touches turns into a miracle. Whatever God deals in, He makes victorious. It's truly amazing, and beyond amazing, how after being bruised, broken, bleeding, and killed, Jesus rose up three days later. Completely healed.

And then a short while later, His disciples witnessed Him drifting into the clouds, ascending into the sky. Going back to the place He came from. Back to being completely connected to His Father forever.

He knows how it feels to be pushed around, rejected, physically and verbally abused. He knows every hurt and pain you will ever feel. Bring those hurts to the One who "gets it." Trust in Him and He will be victorious in your situation. He will bring life into your spirit. He will raise you up, He will heal you completely from every drop of blood that you shed in that place of dark defeat.

Victory over death brings, LIFE.

10

Jesus, the Ultimate Transformer

C an I follow Jesus down the road, of being tortured for things I never did, speaking no defense or anger? When I am blamed and criticized, can I keep my mouth shut instead of trying to prove my point? Can I submit to my Father and die to myself, totally and completely? Can I allow my flesh to be killed, no matter how much it hurts? Can I love when the rest of the world is condemning and mocking? Can I receive hate and give love when I would rather walk away? Can I look at a crowd of people with an unfailing love for each individual heart? Do I hate sin so much that I would risk making people angry, when I rid of it in my house? Can I stop judging by performance or perfection and look at the heart of the person, the root of the matter, and the reason for his actions? Do I love the low-class and underdressed, dirty people as much as I do the wealthy and high-class, clean people? Do I spend as much time with the children as I do the people on my own age level? Can I ask God to forgive those who hate me, while they are spitting on me, torturing me, slamming spikes into my hands and feet, and killing me? Will I be ok when my best friends are not around on the worst night of my life? Will I forgive the one who declared he would die with me, then turns and swears he doesn't know me? Or the one who walked with me every day, now selling me to murderers in exchange for money? When I deserve to be born in a mansion, will a stable be enough? When I have all the knowledge and wisdom to go teach the world, will I be content working as a carpenter, waiting on my Father's timing? When I should be wearing a robe and crown, will my servant clothes be enough? When everyone should be serving me, will I stoop my weary back, bow before them, and wash their crummy feet? When all the world around me bails out on me and does not understand me, will my Father be enough?

Yes, Jesus walked a walk that we cannot even comprehend. His life on earth was all about transformation. He had to come to earth and get into the core of it, to transform it. Everything He touched, changed. Divine Glory colliding with human circumstance caused such a dramatic impact, major change occurred.

John 2:1-10. There was a wedding in Cana of Galilee. And the Mother of Jesus was there. And Jesus and His disciples were called to the marriage. And when they wanted wine, the Mother of Jesus said to Him, "They have no wine." Jesus said unto her, "Woman, what have I to do with thee? Mine hour is not yet come." His mother told the servants, "Whatsoever He saith unto you, do it." And there were set there, six stone water pots after the manner of the purifying of the Jews (the kind used for ceremonial washing) containing twenty or thirty gallons "each." Jesus said to them, "fill the water pots with water." And they filled them up to the brim. That's a large amount of water. Six pots of twenty gallons each is 120 gallons of water. They had their work cut out. Then Jesus said to them, "draw out now, and take it to the governor of the feast." And they took it. When the ruler of the feast had tasted the WATER THAT WAS MADE WINE, and knew not where it came from: (but the servants which drew the water knew) the governor of the feast called the bridegroom, and said unto him, "every man at the beginning sets forth good wine; and when men have well drunk, then he sets forth

that which is worse. BUT THOU HAST KEPT THE GOOD WINE UNTIL NOW."

My water is everything I think is "ok" or "good enough." Anything I settle for, that is less than God intended, is water. Every time I get impatient and choose to do it my way, or if I give up and lose faith, I am choosing my water to stay water. Jesus wants to turn our water into wine. We need to stop trying to make our own wine by trying to turn our own lives into something we think is good. Only Jesus can do that. We need to give Him our water and ask Him to turn it into wine. We need to obey whatever it is He is asking us to do in that process. In the story above, He gave them an assignment. Had they rebelled, or not been faithful enough to do all that tedious work, problems would've occurred. He had the power to do it anyway, but He put them to the test of faith. He does that. He tests our character, what we are made of, how much we really believe Him, by putting us to the test of faith. And then uses that time, of Him working in our situation, to portray His miracle.

Will you let Jesus turn your water into wine? Give Him what you think is good enough or ok. Allow Him to take it and give in return, something far richer and better. By allowing God to take over everything good in your life as well as hard, you are making yourself very vulnerable to change and losing yourself to the most awesome power and the safest place available. God won't do anything with your water until you act out in faith and do with it what He is asking you to. Yes, He could, but He won't. He gave us freedom to choose. He won't force you to fill your water pot then hand it over to Him. If you want to hang on to those stone water pots, afraid of what will happen to them, He will let you. But, you will be missing out on tremendous, and I mean tremendous, blessing and miracles.

With His perfect work in your water, He will turn it into something fuller, richer and much more meaningful. Anything He is invited into, never stays on a shallow level. He takes it to its deepest level, way beyond what we can even dream of. Beyond anything we think is even possible. He does not settle for less. "Good enough," and "ok," He doesn't invest in. There is no limit to His power, His grace, and His ability to do whatever you can't do.

Matthew 14. When Jesus heard of John the Baptist's death, He took a ship and went into a desert place. When the people heard about it, they followed Him on foot out of the cities. When Jesus saw the great multitude, He was moved with compassion toward them and He healed their sick.

Jesus had just found out about John's death. He wanted some time alone, but didn't get that time alone. The people needed Him. He didn't reject them, or turn His back on them, not in the mood. HE WAS MOVED WITH COMPASSION. That is love. Self-sacrificial love that forgets about His own problems when He is needed to help someone else with theirs. It's a love we cannot live without. We need the One who is moved with compassion towards us. The One who gave Himself for us, and came to heal us.

And when it was evening, His disciples came to Him with a big problem. They said, "this is a desert place. The time is now past. Send the multitude away, that they may go into the villages and buy themselves food." It was getting late, and there were thousands of people in an area where there was no food. They were concerned about it and gave their opinion to Jesus. He said to them, "they don't need to depart. Give them something to eat." Imagine their reaction to that one!

Jesus doesn't stop in the middle of a situation. It's easy to think, "well, He's God. He can do anything." True, "but" He was in human flesh. He got weary, hungry, thirsty, and had pain just like we do. He did it anyway. He didn't say, "whew! It's finally evening and time for these people to go home to eat, which is great because finally I get the solo time I so desperately need." No, instead He said, "They don't need to go. Give them food." We all know when we feed someone, they stick around. You want your company to feel welcome and stay awhile, get the food out and you might have to kick them out. Food and socializing go hand in hand.

The disciples said, "we only have five loaves and two fishes." Over five thousand people, and so little food. We would think, "they can cook their own food. I am not prepared for this many people and I'm supposed to feed them. That's just crazy! Plus, I've been here all day. What more can they expect from me?! It's impossible."

But Jesus said, "bring them here to me." And He commanded the multitude to "sit down on the grass." Keep in mind, this is over five thousand people! He took the five loaves and two fishes, and looking up to heaven, He blessed and broke. He gave the loaves to His disciples, and they gave to the multitude. AND THEY ALL ATE, AND WERE FILLED. They took up the fragments that remained and had twelve baskets full.

Jesus wasn't finished with them. He didn't want them to go, so he fed them. They were filled. They didn't scrounge, desperately searching for the last bits. Or barely have enough to make a dent. That day they experienced abundance, straight from the hands of Jesus Himself.

I wish I could've been there. In the middle of the crowd, experiencing it with them. It must've been amazing. The stories these people had to tell their grandchildren, wow!

They obeyed His command and "sat on the grass." Waiting, watching, wondering. Some probably questioned, others doubted, and maybe some laughed. But intently focused on the One who is looking to heaven, they witnessed a miracle. They saw Jesus take all they had, the five loaves and two fishes, and giving back an overflow of food. What was impossible became a reality. Jesus involved.

He eventually did send the multitudes away and went into a mountain to pray. He sent the disciples to go before Him in a ship. He was alone in the mountain. He needed time with His Father. Though He was God, He was in flesh and couldn't minister without His Father's strength. No matter what task we have at hand, responsibility we need to carry out, we are not called to go alone.

That very same night He walked on water. The ship with the disciples was now in the midst of the sea, and tossed with waves, for the wind was contrary. Jesus went unto them, walking on the sea. Have you ever tried to walk on water? You'll end up swimming. When He got in the ship, the wind ceased. And they all worshipped and believed.

When they got across, they came into the land of Gennesaret. When the men there found out about Him, they brought to Him all that were diseased; and besought Him that they might only touch the hem of His garment. AND AS MANY AS TOUCHED WERE MADE PERFECTLY WHOLE.

He wants to do His most perfect work in your heart. Have you besought Him? the word "besought, or beseech" means this: to implore urgently. To beg eagerly for. To beg urgent appeal.

Get involved. Stop believing there is something like being "too serious" about God. God was serious about you before you were even born and He is already extremely involved with you.

Luke 8:22-53. Another chapter of transformation by the Ultimate Transformer.

He calmed a storm. This time He was with them in a ship on a lake. As they sailed, He fell asleep. There came a storm of wind on the lake; and they were filled with water, and were in jeopardy. They woke Him saying, "Master, we perish!" Then He arose, and rebuked the wind and the raging of the water; and they ceased, and THERE WAS A CALM.

There was a man which had devils a long time. He wore no clothes. He did not live in a house, but in the tombs. When he saw Jesus, he cried out and fell down before Him. Jesus asked him his name, and he said, Legion: because many devils were entered into him. The devils besought (begged) Him that He would not command them to go out into the deep. Even the devils cried out for mercy. They begged that He would permit them to go into a herd of pigs feeding on the mountain. And He suffered (permitted) them.

Then the devils went out of the man, and entered into the swine. The herd ran violently down a steep place into the lake, and were choked.

When the people feeding the swine, saw what had happened, they fled, and went and told it in the city and in the country. Then they came to Jesus, and found the man, out of whom the devils were departed, SITTING AT THE FEET OF JESUS, WEARING CLOTHES, AND IN HIS RIGHT MIND.

A man named Jarius, a ruler of the synagogue came and fell down at Jesus' feet, begging Him to come and save his only daughter. She was only twelve, and she was dying.

A woman, bleeding for twelve years, had spent all her money on doctors, and none could heal her. As the people thronged Jesus, she came behind Him and touched the border of His garment. AND IMMEDIATELY, HER BLOOD FLOW STOPPED.

While Jesus was speaking to the woman who touched His garment, a man came to speak to Jarius, saying to him, "your daughter is dead. Do not trouble the Master."

When Jesus heard him, He said, "fear not: BELIEVE ONLY, AND SHE SHALL BE MADE WHOLE." When He came to Jarius' house, all wept and bewailed her. Jesus said, "weep not, she is not dead, but sleeping." They laughed Him to scorn. He put them all out, and took her by the hand, and called, saying, "maid, arise." AND HER SPIRIT CAME AGAIN, AND SHE AROSE IMMEDIATELY.

Transformer, A Man of miracles, the Ultimate and Unfailing. That's who Jesus was, that's who Jesus is.

Saul to Paul, and What Happened in between

Stephen, a man of God, spoke with authority. He spoke the truth. The more he talked, the madder they got. They were furious. Fuming. So angry, they gnashed him with their teeth. He, being full of the Holy Ghost, looked up stedfastly into heaven, and saw the glory of God. He saw Jesus standing on the right hand of God. Stephen then said, "behold, I see the heavens opened, and the Son of man standing on the right hand of God."

The people lost all control. They cried out with a loud voice, covered their ears, and ran upon him with one accord. They stampeded him together. They threw him out of the city and stoned him. The witnesses laid down their clothes at a young man's feet, whose name was Saul. As Stephen was calling upon God saying, "Lord Jesus, receive my spirit," they were throwing the rocks at him in a rage of fury.

Stephen kneeled down, and cried with a loud voice, "Lord, lay not this sin against them."

After pleading for their sin, he died.

The young man named Saul, was giving approval of his death. He was in complete harmony of Stephen's murder.

This young man named Saul, was a troublemaker. He began to destroy the church, dragging off men and women, and committing them to prison. He spoke threats of slaughter against the Lord's disciples. He went to the high priest, and asked him for letters to Damascus to the synagogues, that if he found any followers of Christ, he would capture them and bring them to Jerusalem. He was planning a road-trip. A road-trip full of evil intention. His goal was to wipe out followers of Jesus.

This same young man, wrote 14 books of the Bible. His name is now Paul. His writings in the Bible are full of the Spirit and very powerful. He was an "on fire" man for Christ, and nothing stopped him. He was persecuted and spent many days in prison, writing the Word of God. He did miracles, and converted many people. **Galatians 1:23. He which persecuted the people in times past, now preaches the faith which he once destroyed.** Saul the persecutor, became Paul, the ambassador, the persecuted. People wanted him killed.

What happened between the two identities? What took place that caused such dramatic change?

There is one answer. He had a personal encounter with Jesus Christ, the Son of God. He went on a trip to capture the followers of Jesus, and instead, he became one himself.

In Acts 26:9-18, Paul gives his testimony. This is his story to King Agrippa.

"I indeed thought with myself, that I ought to do many things contrary to the name of Jesus of Nazareth. Which thing I also did in Jerusalem: and many of the saints did I shut up in prison, having received authority from the chief priests, and when they were put to death, I cast my vote against them. I punished them often in every synagogue, and compelled them to blaspheme; and being exceedingly mad against them, I persecuted them even unto strange cities. As I went to Damascus with authority and commission from the chief priests, at midday, O king, I saw in the way A LIGHT FROM HEAVEN, ABOVE THE BRIGHTNESS OF THE SUN, SHINING ROUND ABOUT ME and them which journeyed with me. And when we were all fallen to the earth, I heard a voice speaking unto me, and saying in the Hebrew tongue, "SAUL, SAUL, WHY DO YOU PERSECUTE ME? IT IS HARD FOR YOU TO KICK AGAINST THE PRICKS." AND I SAID, "WHO ARE YOU, LORD?" AND HE SAID, "I AM JESUS WHOM THOU PERSECUTETH. BUT RISE, AND STAND UPON THY FEET: FOR I HAVE APPEARED UNTO THEE FOR THIS PURPOSE, TO MAKE THEE A MINISTER AND A WITNESS OF THESE THINGS WHICH YOU HAVE SEEN, AND OF THOSE THINGS WHICH I WILL SHOW UNTO THEE; DELIVERING THEE FROM THE PEOPLE AND FROM THE GENTILES, UNTO WHOM NOW I SEND THEE. TO OPEN THEIR EYES, AND TO TURN THEM FROM DARKNESS TO LIGHT, AND FROM THE POWER OF SATAN UNTO GOD, THAT THEY MAY RECEIVE FORGIVENESS OF SINS, AND INHERITANCE AMONG THEM WHICH ARE SANCTIFIED BY FAITH THAT IS IN ME."

Whereupon, O king Agrippa, I was not disobedient to the heavenly vision: but shewed first unto them of Damascus, and at Jerusalem, and throughout all the coasts of Judea, and then to the Gentiles, that they should repent and turn to God, and do works meet for repentance. For these causes the Jews caught me in the temple, and went about to kill me. Having therefore obtained help of God, I continue unto this day, witnessing both to small and great, saying none other things than those which the prophets and Moses did say should come: that Christ should suffer, and that He should be the first that should rise from the dead, and should show light unto the people, and to the Gentiles."

Encountered by Jesus, forever changed.

What does this mean for you? You have a story. You have a purpose. Seek His heart and discover.

11

Ruth Marie's Testimony

T his is the story of God's incredible grace, shed upon one soul, that made that one choice.

She is one of my best friends and was for a few years now. Seeing this happen in her life impacted my faith and took it to a whole new level. I had been praying for her, weeping for her, and trying to help her somehow. It broke my heart, seeing how miserable she was and only getting worse. I knew she was so much more than who she was during that time. I'll never forget the moment she told me she accepted Christ. She called me and the second I heard her voice, I knew something had happened. I was so excited, I didn't know what to do with myself. So I did it all. I rejoiced, I cried, I grinned, but mostly I was in complete awe of our God. We were now not only friends, but sisters in Him. It was truly a dream come true. I had been anticipating this, and wanted it to happen so much. Why? Because I knew her heart, and I knew once she surrendered it, He would bring her to incredible places and bring forth an amazing daughter of Him. And that's exactly what He did. Seeing her experience Him was beautiful. He brought incredible, obvious transformation into her life. I saw God break her free from addictions, tearing down strongholds and bondages. She embraced freedom and never looked back. Life poured from her eyes, from the windows to her soul. Her testimony is beautiful, for the art of God in a messy place is nothing less than absolute beauty.

From Her Heart To You

Have you ever felt darkness settle in around you, threatening to take the life inside of you and diminish it completely? As it closes in, any hope of finding peace quickly vanishes instead, leaving you in a pit of anxiety and despair. Your breathing gets harder and you feel like you might suffocate . . . It is then you wonder, "could it get any worse than this?" Somehow, no matter how hard you try to get it right, you always end up here. Here, where "failure" screams your name. A word that tells you you've fallen short once again and as it echoes through your mind, it reminds you of all the other times you messed up.

"Failure." A word I knew well.

It's hard to pin-point exactly when I began believing the lies of the enemy. He does it so slowly and subtly, it's hard to recognize or realize what's happening until it is too late. And then, he's got you trapped.

That's where I found myself one Sunday morning in March. Trapped. Another empty, meaningless weekend had passed and as I sat there on the front porch, with no one else at home, it seemed as though life crashed in around me. There was no more pretending everything was fine, no more wishing "if only I could do this over." For the first time, harsh reality sunk in. The choices I made brought me here. I could never go back and redo it. My past was my past. It breathed down my back and made me want to scream until my lungs went hoarse. But instead, I did the only thing I knew how to do. I picked myself up enough to clean up and face the world again. The weight on my shoulders was heavier . . . the light in my eyes dimmer . . . hopeless . . . and yet, nowhere to turn, it seemed . . .

It wasn't always like this. I grew up as a happy child, a little girl full of hopes and dreams. I learned about Jesus through my family and local Bible school, and asked Him to come into my heart. Several times, actually.

But as I reached my teenage years and peer pressure started raising its ugly head, I saw myself through different eyes. I saw myself as one who never quite reached the expectations of her family, her friends, but most importantly, herself.

I set one goal after another to try and gain self-approval but never could seem to reach any of them. Instead, I'd end up more defeated and more discouraged. There were times I felt hope or excitement for the future, but it was only momentary. An unhealthy cycle of highs and lows became the normal.

As I grew older and started hanging out with friends more often, I discovered rebellion. Doing something "when I clearly knew it was wrong," fed an anger I had developed towards certain people, myself, and God. After all, I had tried pleasing them without success it seemed. And now, sick of trying, I began doing just the opposite.

It came in slowly, listening to music that fed the anger living in my heart. Nothing major, it seemed. But what I didn't realize was the fact that I was doing exactly what the enemy wanted me to do. Step by step, I was walking further into his trap. He is the great deceiver, after all. Convincing you that "you are in control of your life and you can turn back whenever you're tired of playing in sin."

But, how very wrong. It wasn't long before I found myself so far into sin, I didn't know how to get out. Immoral addictions, alcohol, and drugs. Things I "never thought I would do," I was now involved in.

Time and time again I wondered, "is this even worth it? This life." Living seemed unbearable, and yet, I feared death and the possibility of hell too much to end my life. Something had to change.

A few months later, I found myself at a girl's camp. Something my wonderful sister convinced me to go to. "Just get through the weekend," I told myself.

But as one powerful service after another of who God really is, started wrecking the walls of my heart, I got brand new revelation of this God and how wonderful and unconditional His love is towards us. And so during a 3 hour solo time, that hot Saturday afternoon, up on the side of a hill, I surrendered my life to Him. A decision that changed my life. The peace I obtained that day was unlike anything I had ever experienced. Such joy and freedom. What a wonderful, merciful Savior! In that moment, my addictions were held captive because of the blood that washed away all filthiness and gave me a brand new start. Hallelujah!!!

My new challenge and goal is one I know I can reach because "God is on my side." And that goal and challenge is this, "to show His love, the one He showed me when I was in a pit." Portray it to everyone I know, and one day be able to say what Paul said in 2 Timothy 4:7-8. "I have fought a good fight, I have finished my course, I have kept the faith: henceforth there is laid up for me a crown of righteousness which the Lord, the Righteous Judge shall give me at that day: but not to me only, but unto all them also that love His appearing" . . .

A special thank you to Emma Lynn for asking me to share a small part of my story, and also for all the time spent interceding on my behalf.

God bless you . . . Ruthie

12

Me In The Garage

I sit in the garage. Passing time, I just sit there. I'm not really doing anything but sitting where the car normally does, taking its space. I make sounds like a horn and motor. I am doing all the right things to be a car in the garage. I am completely convinced I am a car.

Till one day I wake up and realize I don't have the body of a car, or the engine. I am very void of all it takes to actually be a real car. Sure, I can pretend, imitate, and even brainwash myself of what I am, but the truth is, I am still not a car.

Now on a different level and with new perspective. Are you going to church, pretending you know Jesus and even calling yourself a Christian, but never putting on His body or running on His fuel? Are you doing "all the right things, wearing the right clothes, giving the right amount of money, and following all the rules?" Without even knowing "why."

Why? What is the reason for all that you do? What is the motivation behind all your works? For what cause have you chosen to try and be "good?"

Works by faith are "results" that should come from being in relationship with Christ Himself. The fruit in our lives should be coming forth as a "result" of walking with God. "He" is to be the motivation behind all the good that you do. If it is obligation, making an impression, or proving a point, that is driving you to live a "so called godly life," your works are not based on faith in Him and they are vain. Pointless, empty, and bound to fail. **But we are all as an unclean thing, and all our righteousnesses are as filthy rags; and we all do fade as a leaf; and our iniquities, like the wind, have taken us away. Isaiah 64:6**

Filthy rags here are not just dirty cloths. The translation of this is menstrual cloths. Meaning, the cloths worn during a woman's period. During a woman's period in bible times, she was considered "unclean" and anything she touched became unclean. **Read Leviticus 15:19–27.**

In **Matthew 9** is the story of the woman with the issue of blood for 12 years. Yes, she was physically miserable for 12 years, but it goes far deeper than losing blood. For 12 years she was considered filthy and unclean. According to the law of Moses, anything she would touch became unclean. Her physical disease brought lonliness, rejection, and emotional pain. When Jesus said the life-changing words "your faith has made you whole," it went far beyond stopping the blood-flow. In that moment, He restored her entire being. Physically and emotionally. He gave back to her, all of her life.

Without God as your lifegiver and His righteousness as a result, every work you do is as filthy rags. It is a slippery slope. The enemy will convince you to do good things for all the wrong reasons if he cannot get you to fall. It is so easy to get wrapped up in "what" I'm doing and forget "why" I'm doing it. I get more concerned about putting on a good image to those around me, than the Jesus who saved me. Going to church every Sunday does not make you a Christian any more than sitting in a garage makes you a car. It goes far deeper than showing up at church and doing everything right. Going to church should be a result of your hunger for Christ and your need for fellowship with other believers. It's not just something we "do" on Sunday mornings just because it's "the thing to do." Or is it?

One of the problems with America is not only all the non-Christians and atheists, but all the passive, lukewarm Christians that are warming the bench every Sunday morning in church. The ones that hide behind the tv every other day of the week. The ones that choose to sit back when America needs them to stand up and fight for their families and for what God is calling them to fight for. The ones who tolerate sin in their own houses because they are afraid of their own children. The ones who give up when it gets hard. There is only one who will convince you that you are defeated. It is the enemy. There is only One who fills you with hope and gives you strength to keep fighting when the battle is raging. He brings victory and overcoming. His name is Jesus. Then there are those who think everything is ok. The small backsliders, the little teeny things they forget to guard against because "what's the big deal?" Small things added up, become a heap without you even knowing it. Losing our awareness of sin, is a treacherous path.

If every single person who calls themselves a Christian, would really rise up and take on, to the full extent, what they label themselves to be, this world would be a much better place. There is so much potential in every single heart out there.

God needs to be your source of life. The "reason" you think the things you think, live the way you live, and do all the things you do. He wants this for you because He knows "He" is what is best for you. He has your best interest at heart. He is life-giver, not life-taker. His will is never unhealthy or dangerous. Even if you are in what looks to you like the scariest, most dangerous place in the world, if in the center of His will, you are in the best and safest place to be.

Don't be so concerned about "racking up good points" on God's chart or "doing bad stuff" before you are concerned about building your life on Him. Be more concerned about the Holy Spirit becoming the center and core of your being and who you are. So that it is no longer "you" in you, but "God" in you. Be concerned about making Him your identity, and then your works will be a result. Then be concerned about the fruit you are bringing forth into this world.

For we know that all things work together for good to them that love God, to them who are the called according to His purpose. For whom He did foreknow, (knew beforehand) He also did predestinate (destined in advance) to be conformed to the image of His Son, that He might be the firstborn among many brethren. Moreover whom He did predestinate, them He also called: and whom He called, them He also justified: and whom He justified, them He also glorified. What shall we then say to these things? If God be for us, who can be against us? He that spared not His own Son, but delivered Him up for us all, how shall He not with Him also freely give us all things? Who shall lay anything to the charge of God's elect? It is God that justifieth. Who is he that condemneth? It is Christ that died, yea rather, that is risen again, who is even at the right hand of God, who also maketh intercession for us. Romans 8:28-33

We have been called according to HIS purpose. Not our own. HIS dreams and plans for my life. Not mine. HIS agenda. Not yours. Your creation came with added assignments and tasks for you to accomplish here on earth. He has places prepared for you to pour your passions into. He created you with those passions, therefore, if you seek out the matter, they will fit together uniquely perfect. He gave you all you need to perform the tasks He gives you. And they are uniquely different than anyone else's.

There is the question, "how do I know? What is it He is calling me to do?" As you seek Him, He will reveal it to you, in HIS timing, not yours.

There has been consequences in my life because I refused to heed to the restless feeling in my stomach. I knew it was there but I thought it would go away or I just didn't wanna change my mind. And there were times I didn't feel the stirring, or hear God's voice on my heart, simply because I wasn't listening.

We have also been given the freedom of choice. So if we have the freedom to choose, God won't write our answers in the sky and He seldomly speaks in a loud audible voice. (though many times I have looked up and wished He would) Instead, He speaks to our heart. It's called "gentle, persistent nudging." When you pay attention to that still, small voice, and cry out to Him to speak to your heart and give you assurance, He will. When it is the right time, you will know. Not always immediately. It takes patience, steps of faith, and waiting on God. He sometimes withholds the answer or the full picture so we continue to be helpless and in need of Him. If given an answer immediately, we would automatically, humanly, take it and run with it. Being challenged with unanswered prayer should not bring you to a place of despair, but to a level of greater need and more persistent faith in Him. Acting out on something we feel called to do, but aren't quite positive, requires a whole lot of trust in Him and a big step of faith. It's risky, like stepping over a cliff into the unknown. It's letting go of control and becoming very vulnerable to God's will. There will be times you won't have complete peace or full assurance until after you take a step. Once you do take a risky step of faith over that cliff, God will either give you wings to fly or show you it was the wrong move.

This applies not only to the big stuff in life, but also to all the small daily details. God is a God of protection. He knows exactly what is best for us and what will bring us harm. Therefore He nudges. If we could see the spirit world, we would be amazed the many times we were protected from a car accident etc. by simply taking a different route for some unknown reason. He does it quietly, deep within our soul. If we don't listen or pay attention, we miss out. If you feel a nudge, prompting or stirring, listen to it. If you feel like you just shouldn't go on that trip, buy that house, or send your child to that school, take it to Him. Seek out the matter and pay close attention to it. There's a reason it's there. Most likely He is protecting you from something or directing you to something more fulfilling.

Now back to the question, "how do I know?" The answer lies in PEACE. You will be able to determine what is the right thing, and you will know, by the "peace that passes all understanding." A peace from deep within that only comes from God. A peace that washes over you and takes hold of you, and once you have it, you will know. You just know. It's that simple.

So we, being called to a certain work. Are we willing to be used by God to build His Kingdom? A very wise contractor has made the decision to build a town. Or more like a city. He has the blueprint drawn and the plan mapped out. He knows exactly what He wants done. He knows what needs to be done and has the perfect wisdom to do it, so he decides to do the work himself. The city will be extremely unique with many different projects and parts. So he makes himself thousands of tools, each one different. Each tool he has made can only be used for one thing. His idea will work perfectly with each tool in the desired place. He needs every single tool and gave unique, but very important assignment to each one.

He then tells the tools about his plan and shows them the blueprint. He gives them the ability to choose to co-operate with him and show up on the first day of the job. He has made it very clear to them how much he needs them. He also gave them the freedom to choose whether or not they come.

The big day comes. The contractor is ready to begin putting in place what he has dreamt of. As he waits for the tools to gather around so he can instruct them, he realizes only half have come. Disappointed, but not giving up hope, he uses what's there. The tools are working twice as hard, and trying to do things they haven't originally been designed to do. It's complicated and extremely frustrating. A lot of work gets missed because of a group of lazy tools. The tools that just didn't have time or had some other excuse, complicated and messed up the original plan of the contractor. Had they all come, willing to do exactly what they were designed to do, everything would've fit together and been accomplished the way the contractor originally had in mind.

You've probably already figured it out. The contractor as God, the city His Kingdom, and we are the tools. We are called to be used to build God's Kingdom. Every person with a unique purpose. You, with your talents, gifts, and passions. God put them there to be used by Him to build His Kingdom. Do not fall into the trap of not using your talents. It is God who wants you to use them to glorify Him. It is the enemy who wants to put them to death by getting you to stuff it all in under the carpet, afraid to step out and do something with them. He knows what good can be done with what God gave you, and he fears it. He knows the power in doing what God put you on earth to do, and he hates it. This is why he lies.

Whatever you hear or feel that is hindering you from doing something that will make a difference in another heart, do not listen to that lie. As you listen to the lies, and refuse to use the gifts you have, they will die within you. As you honor God with your gifts and use them, He will bring them to life and give you new oppurtunites and abilities to build His Kingdom. This is extremely important for you to know. So many things keep us from accepting ability God gave us to accomplish things. Fear, insecurity, pride, fear of looking proud, laziness, . . . and so many more.

What God has given you, put it into action and bring it to life. Refuse to let it wither and die within you. It has been given to you for a specific reason. It came with the package of "you" in the moment of your creation.

Now taking another step farther. I came across this scripture and was awestruck.

Shall the axe boast itself against him that heweth therewith? Or shall the saw magnify itself against him that shaketh it? As if the rod should shake itself against them that lift it up, or as if the staff should lift itself up as if it were no wood. Isaiah 10:15

I was picturing exactly what it is saying and it's quite comical. Imagine an axe bragging that he cut down a tree when he can't even swing himself, a chainsaw saying he cut the wood when he has no power to even start himself or the staff telling the world how he picked himself up. And the city, where the tools couldn't do a thing without the contractor picking them up and using them. After the city was all built, or even during construction, how pathetic if they had boasted to their neighbors about the project they were doing.

Again, this is us. We have been given gifts, but they have been put there by our Creator. We cannot, for one second, boast against Him that moves us. We are only tools, but we are tools. Made available, He will use us. Using us, He gets the glory and the credit. Every ounce of it.

13

The Battle. Spirit VS Flesh

There is a raging battle going on. Through every day of your life, with every breath you breathe, you are being fought over by two very powerful forces. God versus Satan. They both want your soul. They are both pursuing your heart and will do what it takes to win you. One desires to put you to death, the Other desires to bring you to life.

There was once a beautiful young woman married to a warrior man. He loved her so much and valued her heart. He had rescued her from the outside world by risking his life for her. He was now extremely committed to her and offered her a lifetime of peace and deep joy. He pursued her and fought for her heart every day. He made himself a one woman man and became trustworthy. His heart belonged only to her. He gave it all for her. She was his purpose and reason for life. He built a house and provided for her all she needed. He protected her and became her safe place emotionally and physically. He kept all her secrets and never broke his promises. He built a shelter for her heart where it was safe for her to be open and vulnerable to him. A place where she could thrive and be all the woman she was created to be.

Midst all this glory and bliss came challenges. There were daily responsibilities that came with being married. Money was tight at times. Work needed to be done even when she was tired. Her warrior man asked her to walk with him into places that took effort and surrender. Because she was married and committed, her entire life changed. Her schedule became theirs. Her choices weren't just her own anymore. For the marriage to reach its deepest level and for her to experience all of complete fulfillment, the journey of submitted, unconditional love needed to be trod. But even in the midst of the challenges, she "knew" this was what she wanted.

There came a day when a neighbor moved in across the street. The moment she saw him, she remembered him from the raging outside world her warrior man had rescued her from. She had always been tempted by him and at one point, she had even thought she loved him. There was something alluring and even attractive about him. After she was rescued, she saw the trap for what it was, therefore she knew he was dangerous. So she chose to ignore him and not allow herself to go there.

However, the instant he noticed her, he also remembered and wanted her back. He knew she was married and committed. He knew going over and asking her out wouldn't work. So he decided to do it the sly and quiet way. In ways that she would barely notice but with enough suction to lure her to him. He knew her likes and weaknesses for he had spent a good amount of time with her in the past. He started by making himself look good and becoming attractive. And then he hung around, walking the streets, passing her house, just being around. He knew her need for affirmation and communication. He knew how much she loved to talk and how much she appreciated flowers. So he did all these things little by little.

She barely even noticed herself reacting at first. She soon was convinced he was ok to have around, nothing was happening between them. He was just a friendly neighbor. What happened in the past was staying in the past. What started in small became bigger. The minute her husband left for work, he came by and stayed until just before he came home. The more attached she got to him, the more discontent she was with her warrior man. This was now affecting their marriage. Eventually he declared his love for her and promised her an easy life of freedom and happiness. No work, no commitment, just fun and freedom. He spent money on her and started competing with her husband. He wasn't keeping it a secret anymore. She was now involved with him and he was willing to openly pursue her. He intentionally offered her a better life, wooing her away from her sanctuary of beautiful safety.

And where was her husband? He was at war. He was fighting with all he had. He bought locks for every door and window in the house, and continued to provide for her. He protected her and pursued her harder than ever before. He never stopped loving her and never gave up on her heart. When neighbor guy came over, he got out the weapons and fought, risking his life once again for her. The more he fought, the more the neighbor guy fought. This became a daily battle between two men. One man who would die for her to bring her life, and one man who would take from her whatever he could, then destroy her. One man who loved her. One man who loved himself.

As her husband fought, he loved. As he loved, he fought. He knew the neighbor guy all too well. He knew about the lies and what would happen to his beloved if she went away with him. Thinking about losing her to his enemy broke his heart. Not only because of losing her, but also because he knew she would die, and that is what drove him to fight. He continued to fight because she needed him to. The enemy was much stronger than her, and could snatch her in his pursuit if she was alone. Therefore she needed an intercessor, a warrior man, someone who would never stop fighting for her.

With this powerful force of love that drove warrior man to fight hard, came something else. Her freedom to choose between the two at battle. Because he loved her so much he could not force her to stay with him. Unconditional love brings forth the result of giving to the other, the freedom to choose to love in return. If there is force, it is not love. It is obsession or control.

So every day he gave her a choice. As the enemy circled the house, calling her name in deceiving charm, begging her to come away with him, her husband gazed steadfastly into her eyes, penetrating the deepest parts of her soul. In the most heartbreaking and the riskiest moment of the day, he said to her with tears streaming down his face, "my beloved, I will fight as long as you want me to. And even when you don't want me to, I will fight. I will never stop fighting for you. With all my heart I want you to stay here with me. I know how destroyed you will be with him and it tears me apart knowing what he will do to you. But right now I give you the freedom to choose. Right now, the decision is up to you. I have every power to defeat him and I will, if that is what you want."

This story is us every single day. We are being fought over by two spirits of pursuit. One who is destructive and One who is life-giving. One who loves you and died for you and one who hates you and wants you to go down with him. Understanding this, it makes so much more sense why we struggle the way we do. Why so many times we know what we really want, we know what is safe and right, but our flesh is so pathetically weak. The spirit is willing but the flesh is weak. This is why we need a fighter, a warrior God. We cannot fight the battle alone. Without God fighting this battle for us, we will get swept off our feet in the enemy's lures.

I grew up with a brother that goes trapping, hunting, and fishing, and I've joined in on the fishing a few times. I learned what it takes to "get something" in all 3 of these categories. Bait or lure is one. Use something the animal or fish loves to feed on. Attract it with something its flesh craves. Keeping your scent away and disguising is another. Make as little movement as possible. Camouflage so they can't see you.

A skilled hunter will make a dangerous and fatal area look safe and life-giving. A trap well hidden brings an end result of death. The animal is lured, deceived, manipulated, tricked, and then killed.

This is exactly how the enemy works. He will never show you the end result. He will only make it look good for now. He disguises evil and makes it look good because he knows, we, in the likeness of God, desire good. We are not attracted to ugly or something that looks like death. Most likely we will steer clear of anything in that likeness. This is why he wears the heaviest camouflage. He sets traps and hides them well. He puts down lures and covers his own tracks. The end result is destruction. He doesn't give the real deal. Only God has that to offer. The enemy gives what to our tunnel vision "looks" like the real deal, but is only a fake.

How do we know the traps? What is a lure? What is from the Holy Spirit? How do I discern good and evil? One way. Through Jesus Christ, and putting on His mind. Without Him on our side and showing us, we will never know. And yes, we will be ensnared by the traps. We will be vulnerable to all that "looks" good. We will be gullible and narrow minded, without wisdom. In a relationship with Him, He will reveal to you His truth. Spending time in His word brings wisdom, understanding, and firm standing against the lures of the enemy. You need Him desperately. Again I say, desperately. You need Him to fight for you. You need Him to wake up your soul and bring you awareness of the enemy's destructive snares. He will come through for you, because He loves you. He will speak to you in your spirit and give you clearer perspective, if you LISTEN TO WHAT HE HAS TO SAY. The only way you will ever know the difference between good and evil, is through Him speaking that truth into your life. The dimmer His voice, the louder the enemy's. And the enemy is speaking filthy lies covered in a fake, deceiving something that only "looks" beautiful. After Paul's life radically changed, he didn't suddenly "stop" struggling. That's when the real battle began. Prior to his encounter with Jesus he was only listening to one voice. Once he began hearing the voice of God, there was major conflict. In **Romans 7 and 8** he shares his struggles.

"For I know that in me (that is, in my flesh) dwells no good thing. For too will is present with me; but how to perform that which is good I find not. For the good that I would, I do not: but the evil which I would not, that I do. Now if I do that

I would not, it is no more I that does it, but sin that dwells in me. I find then a law, that, when I would do good, evil is present with me. For I delight in the law of God after the inward man: but I see another law in my members, warring against the law of my mind, and bringing me into captivity to the law of sin which is in my members. Oh wretched man that I am! Who shall deliver me from the body of this death? I THANK GOD THROUGH JESUS CHRIST OUR LORD. So then with the mind I myself serve the law of God. But with the flesh the law of sin." There is therefore now no condemnation to them which are in Christ Jesus, who walk not after the flesh, but after the Spirit. For the law of the Spirit of life in Christ Jesus hath made me free from the law of sin and death. For what the law could not do, in that it was weak through the flesh, GOD SENDING HIS OWN SON IN THE LIKENESS OF SINFUL FLESH, AND FOR SIN, CONDEMNED SIN IN THE FLESH: that the righteousness of the law might be fulfilled in us, who walk not after the flesh but after the Spirit. For they that are after the flesh do mind the things of the flesh; but they that are after the Spirit the things of the Spirit. For to be unspiritually minded is death, but to be spiritually minded is life and peace. Because the unspiritual mind is enmity against God: for it is not subject to the law of God, neither in deed can be. So then they that are in the flesh cannot please God. But ye are not in the flesh, but in the Spirit, IF SO BE THAT THE SPIRIT OF GOD DWELL IN YOU. NOW IF ANY MAN HAVE NOT THE SPIRIT OF CHRIST, HE IS NONE OF THIS. And if Christ be in you, the body is dead because of sin, but the Spirit is life because of righteousness. BUT IF THE SPIRIT OF HIM THAT RAISED UP JESUS FROM THE DEAD DWELL IN YOU, HE THAT RAISED UP CHRIST FROM THE DEAD SHALL ALSO GIVE LIFE TO YOUR MORTAL BODIES BY HIS SPIRIT THAT DWELLS IN YOU. Therefore brethren, we are debtors, not to the flesh, to live after the flesh. **For if ye live after the flesh, ye shall die: BUT IF YE THROUGH THE SPIRIT PUT TO DEATH THE DEEDS OF THE BODY, YE SHALL LIVE. FOR AS MANY AS ARE LED BY THE SPIRIT OF GOD, THEY ARE THE SONS OF GOD.**

Here Paul is speaking of his flesh and the power of the sin in his flesh. The point he really brings out though is this, **"without Jesus Christ dwelling in me, I will die."** He is recognizing and acknowledging his desperate need for a God who is fighting for him. He knows he needs an intercessor, someone to come through for him, a Warrior God, because alone, he is a pathetic, lost, flesh-driven soul.

How do we separate the flesh from the Spirit, remove sin and replace it with godliness? And what about those desires that stick around even after committing to Christ, counting the cost of following Him, and being willing to do whatever it takes? It's like you know what you really want but your flesh keeps playing tricks on you.

God works powerfully in many different ways. One of these is, He fights for us. Another is, He gives us what it takes to walk away or say no in a situation of being tempted and tried. But we have that choice to make, every single time. It is called "being intentional" or doing it "on purpose." By choosing commitment to Christ, there comes along with that, new responsibilities, challenges, and hard choices to make.

He won't knock a bottle of whiskey out of an alcoholics hand by some magical force, or burn the destructive magazines in an addicts house. But He provides every strength needed to do it.

Walking away or stopping a bad habit needs to be done by you. You are the one who needs to get a grip on what is controlling you. And the only way you can do it, is if you are completely in need of the Only One who will show you how. On your own, it is impossible to get a grip and stop.

A desire will not go away as long as you keep feeding it. Yes, your desires are transformed and renewed by walking with Christ, but your flesh will not go away and the enemy does not give up that quick. You must starve your flesh to kill the desire. The flesh is never satisfied. The more it gets, the more it wants.

It is the same with Spiritual desire. For it to deepen or grow, you must keep feeding it with Spiritual food. If you stop feeding your Spiritual hunger or desire, it will fade off and change into a desire of the flesh.

We are created for extreme passion and thrill. Our souls will always be yearning for something deep and exciting. You will always have desire. It is not wrong, only beautiful and very valuable. Never stop desiring or having fiery passion. It is life-giving. It is only "what" you crave and are passionate about that is destructive.

Do you find yourself frustrated with your flesh? You have guilt burning in the pit of your stomach and your flesh keeps wanting more. You're disappointed in yourself because the last time was gonna be "the last time." With the flesh, there is no last time. With the Holy Spirit involved, there is a last time.

When I was younger, there was a stray cat around our house. A skinny, sick-looking cat. The first time I saw it, I took pity on it and could not chase it away. I left it hang around, hoping it would leave soon. It didn't. Instead it followed me, whining and meowing. As it cried I felt more sorry for it, so I finally gave in and fed it. Satisfied for a while, the cat left. The next night, at the same time in the same place, there it was. Once again it was hungry, and it refused to leave until I fed it. This was a repeated deal for a few nights and eventually it stopped coming. If I had not fed it that first night, I would've never seen it again. But because I kept feeding it, thinking, "one more time," it kept returning.

Desire of the flesh is just like that. Sin is like that. We cannot hang around something and think we won't be affected. If we allow the temptation to linger, hoping it goes away, eventually our flesh does give in. Temporary satisfaction is what we experience. We feel completely satisfied, thinking "never again." It then digests, passes through, and we are hungry again.

If your flesh has a hold on you in any way, even what you think might just be something small and no big deal, but deep down you really want freedom, believe and know it is available. Don't give up, defeated. Rise up with new strength. Cry out to God for deliverance. Bring Him into those areas and ask Him to take over. Be ready and willing to change your desires and He will give you grace and every strength you need to say no. He will provide a way out of the situations and places where you have been trapped in the past.

With Him there is a walk to walk, and a lifestyle to adapt to, and no it is not easy, because every single moment we are being fought over in a ferocious battle. God vs the enemy.

Don't put up with your flesh and the enemy. Don't tolerate defeat and failure. Instead, do whatever it takes to be victorious in Jesus Christ. You have a choice. Every single moment.

14

The Heart Of Worship

For ye shall go out with joy and be led forth with peace. The mountains and the hills shall break forth before you into singing and all the trees of the field shall clap their hands. Instead of the thorn, shall come up the fir tree, and instead of the brier shall come up the myrtle tree, and it shall be to the Lord for a name, for an everlasting sign that shall not be cut off. Isaiah 55:12-13

How can anyone see nature, be in it, experience it, or even just get a taste of it and not "know" there is a mighty Hand behind it all? How could anyone possibly think it "just happened?" How meaningless, dried up and so not romantic.

God speaks through all He has created. Not only speaks, but passionately pursues us with the works of His hands. His soul cries out to us in the vast sunrise. His heart is beating upon the earth in the moonlit sky. He longs to get our attention, therefore He uses beauty. Beauty that no artist, painter, or professional designer can even come close to.

Last night we witnessed and experienced a sky different than I had ever seen before. First it was the colors. As the sun dipped below the horizon, colors beyond description filled the sky. It was as if there was a giant paintbrush being swept across the vast open sky. And then as the sky got dark, the moon came out. It was a partly cloudy night which made it breathtaking. The moon behind the clouds cast rays and silver linings all over the edges of the clouds. It was stunning. It was perfect. It was God. It was my Father wooing me, pursuing me, urging me to get into His heart.

What better way to steal someone's heart than giving them something that leaves them breathless? There is a pull there. Something about nature yanks at our heartstrings in a deep, indescribable way. I often wondered why. And then I got a few answers. Every time I am at the beach, in the mountains, walking in our back fields, or watching a sunset, I feel at home. Everything feels right in that very moment. It can be a crazy chaotic time in my life, but in the midst of nature, surrounded by the heart of God, everything is ok. All is well.

Why? We are created for this. We are designed to be captivated by all nature. It's God's way of bringing us back to Him. Walk a busy street in the middle of the city and it's hard to hear the whisper of God on your heart. But get yourself in a forest, on the beach with no one around, or on the bay at sunset, and it's hard to get distracted from the serenity of it all. You will want to stay that way forever.

We are created for heaven. We long for something beautiful because that is exactly what God is preparing for us. We were not made to enjoy mud and dry barren fields. The lush green, and deep colors is our desire, because that is what all of heaven will be and that is where the heart of God pumps at its loudest.

We are a part of the creation. In the deepest, most vital part of our heart and soul, we have a connection and relation with nature. It is perfect harmony because we have the same Maker. We belong to the same God. The same hands that formed the mighty seas and the rocky mountains, the perfect wildflower breaking free from the cold winter ground, are the hands that formed you and me.

Nature is alive. Everything God touches is life. Ponder creation and you will see life by breath, growth, or movement. Birds and animals breathe, trees and plants grow, and there is movement to many things. The earth rotates. The waters move, clouds float, and on and on. Life, energy, excitement. This is our God.

Have you ever noticed how nature worships? Nature sings out in worship. Everything has a purpose and they all do it in a form of worship. The night sounds in the middle of the summer are incredible. The birds, the sound of the water and again, on and on . . . But worship is not always making noise. The parts of nature that don't make a sound are still in complete worship. Because they are doing exactly what they are created to do. The maple tree isn't worried about what it will do the next day, stressed about its schedule and the fact that all its leaves will die soon. It's got roots planted deep into the heart of the earth. The birds don't care that they sing the same song over and over again. They are just being what they are made to be, doing what they are called to do, with life and beauty, and in joy and submission to their Maker.

Nature, just being and doing, WITH ALL ITS HEART, IN FULL AND COMPLETE WORSHIP.

So really, what is worship? It is a way of connecting with our Maker, or being connected to Him. Getting into the heart of God, is our heart in worship. It is either "doing" or "being," or both. Worship is a form of praise, adoration, honor, glorifying, or deeply loving. The truest form of worship is the state of "being." It is a position of the heart. You can be in full and complete worship without uttering a word.

There's a few different descriptions or meanings of worship in the Bible. The Hebrew word, "shachah," means "prostrate, to bow down, crouch, fall down, humbly beseech, do reverence."

The Greek word, "proskuneo," means "to kiss like a dog licking his master's hand, to crouch to, do reverence to, adore."

The Greek word, "sebomai," means "to reverence, hold in awe, to feel awe, whether before God or man." The Greek word in **Luke 14:10**, "doxa," means, "glory, honor, praise, of good reputation, an appearance commanding respect." Only once in the Bible does the word "worship" mean "doxa." Most times the words "glory, praise or honor" are used for "doxa." I encourage you to look up **Luke 14:10**. It has a very interesting meaning of worship. Studying these words, I was amazed.

The Greek word, "letreuo," means "to serve, to render religious service of homage to."

The Greek word, "eusebeo," means "to be pious toward, to respect, reverence." Worship is also only used once for this word in the Bible. It's found in **Acts 17:23**.

The Greek word "ethelothreskeia" is found in **Colossians 2:23** and it's the only place it's found in the Bible. It means "voluntarily adopted worship, not that which is imposed by others, but which one affects himself."

The English word, "worship" means "to literally ascribe worth to something."

Many times, or most times in the Bible when people had an encounter with Jesus, they worshipped. (unless they hated Him)

The disciples and the two Marys worshipped Him when seeing Him for the first time after His resurrection. Job had a heart of worship. He was the greatest of all the men of the east and lost his ten children, seven thousand sheep, three thousand camels, five hundred yoke of oxen, five hundred donkeys, in a moment. What's amazing here is the way Job reacted. He arose, tore his clothes, shaved his head, and then fell down upon the ground and WORSHIPPED. He said, "naked came I out of my Mother's womb, and naked shall I return there. The Lord gave, and the Lord has taken away. BLESSSED BE THE NAME OF THE LORD." Then after He worshipped and continued to love God, Satan smote Job with sore boils, (inflamed, painful, pus-filled swellings on the skin) from the bottom of his feet to the top of his head. He used a piece of pottery to scrape himself, and he sat down among the ashes. His wife told him to curse God and die, and he replied, "what? Shall we receive good at the hand of God, and not evil?" IN ALL THIS JOB DID NOT SIN WITH HIS LIPS. The scripture continues with Job being miserable. His friends came to visit but couldn't speak to him, for they saw his grief was great. Job lamented, cursed the day he was born, he wept, he mourned, he wanted die, for he was in complete torture. But he never stopped loving God and holding Him high above himself. His heart was in a position of worship the entire time. The result, the Lord gave Job twice as much as he had before, and blessed the latter end more than his beginning.

After Job lost everything, He did the unthinkable in our time. He lost it all. His riches, and his health, yet he REFUSED to turn away from God. In his anguish he believed in a Higher understanding than his own. Even though he didn't "get it" he knew God did.

What does worship mean for you? Does the presence of the Almighty cause you to fall prostrate at His feet? Do you ever look to the heavens and hold a deep reverence for the One you have encountered? Or do you go about your daily life, never really taking the time to worship, to lift Him high above yourself and the day you are living in?

If you desire a closer, more intimate walk with Him, worship is a vital and very necessary part of your journey. Getting before your Maker, no matter what the circumstance, is a major part of your relationship with Him. Adoring Him, loving Him, simply bringing your heart into connection with His, is marrow to your bones. Without it, they will become brittle, hollow, and they will break. It is life to your soul and spirit. Again, worship is not only doing something. It is a position of the heart. What you do is a result of what's happening inside. It is possible to be in the heart of worship throughout the day, at any time. Worship means having a heart of complete reverence to Him and being in awe of Him. Living in worship does not mean, praising Him for an hour, and then forgetting about what happened in that hour. If it's real, it will go with you. This is why it is so important to spend time with Him alone, daily. To get connected with Him, get into the heart of worship and then take it with you wherever you go and into whatever you do. Worship is a wide realm and mixture of action and being. We need to take action and be intentional. Don't try to do it according to your own strength or try to "get yourself a heart of worship." That never works. Ask God Almighty to fill you with what He has to fill you with. Ask Him to pour ultimate worship into every part of your being. Beg Him to give you a heart of worship for Him. As He fills you up, react and do act of worship. Even when you're not feeling it, take action. Choose to praise anyway. That brings beautiful results. And then there's the "just being" area in the realm of worship. Being in awe of Him. Being still and quiet in His presence. It is simply being connected to Him, completely wrapped up in Him, without really doing anything but thinking on Him, appreciating His presence, and giving Him glory.

Worship comes easy when all is good and well. Especially in an area of complete beauty or surrounded by stunning nature. My heart fills to the brim at those times. I feel so overwhelmed with love and adoration in those deep moving moments.

But what about the tough days? When everyone around is annoying, or I'm "just not in the mood?" The days you feel exhausted the second your feet hit the floor and you have a million tasks to accomplish that day. The times of trial, disappointment, or loss. Is it possible to be in reverence and awe of God and actually appreciate the work He is doing in those worst case scenerios? The day you overslept and it all started wrong, the boss is in a bad mood, the children are sick and you really, really wanted to go to that party, your car gives out and your account is already headed towards empty. The little annoying stuff that can become a heap of despair or the times in your life, like Job, you lost it all. Those moments in time when you feel like you just can't think positive right now.

Yes, it is possible. By choosing to hold God in His place and continuing to be in worship of Him, He brings you back to Himself. To a place way beyond the circumstance. A place where the power of the situation lessens and He is magnified in your heart. A place where it's ok if you don't understand because you know "He does." Pressure of performance or having it all together fades out when you are in the heart of worship. Because when we lift up our hearts to Him, reach out our souls in genuine worship, it is then heaven reaches down, captivates our hearts, and saturates every situation that has become a barrier or hindrance to the heart of God. It is then no longer you bearing it all, but God bearing it all, giving you reason to believe again. It is then you are doing exactly what you have been created to do. Being connected to His heart and living out a heart of worship.

Why Worship?

Oh come, let us sing unto the Lord, let us make a joyful noise to the Rock of our salvation. Let us come before His presence with thanksgiving, and make a joyful noise unto Him with psalms. FOR THE LORD IS A GREAT GOD, AND A GREAT KING ABOVE ALL GODS. IN HIS HAND ARE THE DEEP PLACES OF THE EARTH, THE STRENGTH OF THE HILLS IS HIS ALSO. THE SEA IS HIS AND HE MADE IT, AND HIS HANDS FORMED THE DRY LAND. Oh come, let us worship and bow down, let us kneel before the Lord our Maker. FOR HE IS OUR GOD AND WE ARE THE PEOPLE OF HIS PASTURE AND THE SHEEP OF HIS HAND. Today, if you will hear His voice. Psalm 95 Oh sing unto the Lord a new song, sing unto the Lord all the earth. Sing unto the Lord, bless His name, show forth His salvation from day to day. Declare His gory among the heathen, His wonders among all people. FOR THE LORD IS GREAT, AND GREATLY TO BE PRAISED. HE IS TO BE FEARED ABOVE ALL GODS. FOR ALL THE GODS OF THE NATIONS ARE IDOLS, BUT THE LORD MADE THE HEAVENS. HONOUR AND MAJESTY ARE BEFORE HIM, STRENGTH AND BEAUTY ARE IN HIS SANCTUARY. Give unto the Lord the glory due unto His

name. Oh worship the Lord in the beauty of holiness. Let the heavens rejoice, let the earth be glad, let the sea roar and the fullness thereof. Let the field be joyful, and all that is therein, then shall all the trees of the wood rejoice before the Lord; FOR HE COMETH TO JUDGE THE EARTH. HE SHALL JUDGE THE WORLD WITH RIGHTEOUSNESS, AND THE PEOPLE WITH HIS TRUTH. Psalm 96.

On and on . . . throughout Psalms, it's praise, it's worship. Worship that goes beyond the outward circumstances of today. Real, authentic worship coming from a heart that knows the truth. A worship that goes far beyond human understanding. A worship that draws the heart nearer to God's heart than ever before.

Reading over these Psalms, I get the idea there's One reason for the worship going on. One reason the heavens, the earth and everything therein rejoice. The core reason is none other than God Himself.

Have you ever felt like heaven is right here? Have you ever been so wrapped up in the presence of God that you weren't sure where He ended and you started? It was He in you and you in Him all mixed together. That was worship in the state of being. It was that moment in time when all else faded away. You were in complete awe of Him who set you free. HIM WHO SET YOU FREE. HIM WHO SET YOU FREE. HIM WHO SET YOU FREE.

Feel it with the rhythm of your beating heart, HIM WHO SET YOU FREE. HIM WHO SET YOU FREE. HIM WHO SET YOU FREE . . .

And this is why we worship. This is why worship is so important. Coming into the heart of worship brings us to a realization of who God really is and what He has done for us. With that comes a new appreciation and a heart of overflowing gratitude, NO MATTER WHAT IS HAPPENING OUTWARDLY. God will always be God, and His salvation will never leave.

For He will light your candle. The Lord your God will bring light into your dark places. He will give you strength

to run through a troop, and leap over walls. As for God, HIS WAY IS PERFECT. The word of the Lord is proven. He is a shield to all those that trust in Him. For who is God except the Lord? Who is a Rock except our God? It is God that girds you with strength, and makes your way perfect. He makes your feet like deer's feet and sets you up on high places. He teaches your hands to war, so that a bow of steel is broken by your arms. HE HAS ALSO GIVEN YOU THE SHIELD OF HIS SALVATION, and His right hand has held you up, and His gentleness has made you great. He has enlarged your steps under you, that your feet did not slip. Psalm 18:28-36

Yes, we are called to worship. We are called to honor and adore the King, passionately and wholeheartedly. Because He has made Himself known to us and has made a way for us to overcome sin. He has made us conquerors and victorious through the blood of Jesus. He has chosen us to be set free and to be transformed into all He desires us to be. Many reasons, but they all boil down to one event. Jesus' death and resurrection. SALVATION. What happened on the cross is the reason we worship.

God created you and me with different ways of connecting with His heart. He gave us different interests, passions and ways of getting intimate with Him. He has certain ways of making your heart skip a beat that are unique to the rest of the world. He has a way of making adrenaline pump through you. He uses things to get you back to Himself that are different than anyone else He created. He, in His infinite mind and heart, has a way of "clicking" with every single human being in a unique, individual way. This is His heart of romance. He knows what you love and what brings you to a sense of awe, and those are the things He is using to win your heart. Pay attention. That feeling, that emotion that sets your heart on fire, He has put it there. Gently, passionately, and perfectly.

Jesus said to the woman at the well, "but the hour cometh and now is, when the true worshippers shall worship the Father in Spirit and in truth, FOR THE FATHER SEEKETH SUCH

TO WORSHIP HIM. God is a Spirit and they that worship Him, must worship Him in Spirit and in truth." John 4:23-24

Right now, you are the one at the well. Jesus is asking you, calling you, to worship the Father. Him, in His righteousness, truth, glory, majesty and Holiness is calling you out to step forward and find reason to worship. Just as the earth breaks forth in true worship and as Job did, can you, as His beloved child, react in the same way? Can you live in true, authentic, deep and passionate worship for no reason other than THE GREATNESS OF HIM AND THE GIFT OF SALVATION? Can His greatness intrigue you and drive you to be in complete awe of Him, day in and day out, no matter what is happening in your life right now?

Take a close look at your worship life. Open your heart to His heart. Ask Him to reveal to you what sets your heart on fire. He will show you how to connect with Him. He will romance you and win you. He will show you what you are truly passionate about and when He does, do not set a limit in that place of your soul. Boundaries are dangerous when being intimate with Christ. Go all the way. Step out with courage and give it all to the One who gave it all for you.

Afterword

eader, THANK YOU for taking the time to read what God has put on my heart to share with you. My prayer is that you have a new desire for your King. I pray you are hungry and thirsty for Him and for all He has to offer you. Oh, He loves you so much. And He has so much in store for you right now. Right now, in this very moment, He has purpose for you. He believes in His beloved. He has a work for you. And most importantly, He wants your heart. Yes, your heart surrendered to Him and washed clean by His flowing blood. He has made it available for you. Are you afraid of this truth or will you allow it to set you free? I know the feeling. I have dealt with it and still do at times. Giving it all up to Christ is way too much like losing control. But I have learned He is a whole lot more trustworthy than I myself am. He is much more careful with my heart than I myself am. My heart in His hands is safe, but if I choose to keep it in my own hands, it is in danger. By choosing to let go and fully trust in His unfailing strength, life becomes rich and meaningful. Eternity loses its vagueness and becomes real. Things begin to make sense and pieces come together. The future and death hold hope and excitement, instead of fear and dread. Yes, He is preparing a place for you. Yes, He is returning for those who have chosen to receive Him. Again, thank you for taking the time to read. You are loved and appreciated. May God bless you abundantly, may His face shine upon you, and may He be gracious to you with every beat of your heart . . .

Emma Lynn

CPSIA information can be obtained at www.ICGtesting.com
Printed in the USA
BVOW04s1909310114

343500BV00001BA/23/P

9 781462 727728